EVERYMAN'S
BIBLE
COMMENTARY

FIRST & SECOND
PETER

EVERYMAN'S
BIBLE
COMMENTARY

FIRST & SECOND
PETER

Lou Barbieri

MOODY PUBLISHERS
CHICAGO

Scripture quotations are taken from the *New American Standard Bible®*, © Copyright The Lockman Foundation 1960, 1962, 1963, 1968, 1971, 1972, 1973, 1975, 1977, 1995. Used by permission.

Scripture quotations marked KJV are taken from the *King James Version.*

Library of Congress Cataloging-in-Publication Data

Barbieri, Louis.
    First & Second Peter / Lou Barbieri.
       p. cm.— (Everyman's Bible commentary)
    Originally published: Chicago : Moody, © 1975.
    ISBN 0-8024-2110-5
    1. Bible. N.T. Peter—Commentaries. I. Title: First and Second Peter. II. Title. III. Series.

BS2795.53.B37 2003
226'.9207—dc21
                                    2003007414

1 3 5 7 9 10 8 6 4 2

Printed in the United States of America

To my three children:

Joanne

You were "pure joy" to your mother and me,
and you are already enjoying
the glories of heaven with our beloved Savior.

Jeff

You have been our quiet, strong, second child,
and because of your love for God's Word we are confident
that He will continue to use you significantly for His glory.

Jason

You have kept your mother and me young in heart,
and we admire your spiritual sensitivity and openness
to God's continual leading in your life and ministry.

*I love you all and thank God
for what He has taught me through you!*

CONTENTS

PREFACE TO THE
REVISED EDITION

My heart greatly rejoiced when the first edition of this Everyman's Bible Commentary on 1 and 2 Peter became available, for it was my first published work. I never dreamed that this book would still be in print more than twenty-five years after it first appeared. I am thankful to the Lord that apparently many readers are still finding that the work answers some of their questions about Peter's books and that it continues to minister to people.

When the commentary was originally published, it was based on the Authorized Version of the Scripture, better known as the King James Version. This was the version I was using when I began my teaching ministry at the Moody Bible Institute. It was about the time of the publication of this commentary that I began to become more familiar with the *New American Standard Bible* (NASB). Although I still love the Authorized Version, I found that the NASB would more often than not communicate the Greek text in a way that was clearer to my audiences. I found myself explaining many words in the English AV text that were already printed in the text of the NASB. I came to the conclusion that I was spending more time teaching English than I was teaching Bible. It has therefore been my desire for some time to make some changes in this commentary and to utilize the NASB text. I am very thankful that when I approached the editors at Moody Publishers with this idea, they were favorable to the change.

Therefore you now have in your hands a revised edition of the Everyman's Bible Commentary that is based on the NASB. It has still been my goal to comment on every verse in the two books written by the apostle Peter. While I do not expect that every reader will agree with every conclusion I have come to, this commentary will at least give you a position to wrestle with. I trust as you read these pages and interact with other Scriptures you will "grow in the grace and knowledge of our Lord and Savior Jesus Christ" (2 Peter 3:18). Truly to Him alone does belong all the glory.

MEET PETER

1

PETER THE MAN

Of the many individuals portrayed in the pages of the Holy Scriptures, the apostle Peter is outstanding. We are drawn to him because he was so typically human, and we can identify with his successes and failures. Peter was the kind of person who had an opinion on every subject and expressed it on every occasion. His forcefulness caused him to appear forward—and even rash.

On the positive side, Peter was eager, energetic, self-confident, daring, aggressive, hopeful, bold, and courageous. But, like most of us, Peter had a negative side to his character. At times before Christ's ascension, Peter was also fickle, weak, impulsive, cowardly, inconsistent, and sometimes unstable.

Who was this man whom the Lord called to be an apostle? Why did he change? What experiences influenced him?

HIS BACKGROUND

NAME AND FAMILY

Although this apostle is known primarily by the name Peter, his given name was Simon, or more properly, Simeon (John

1:40–42). "Simeon" is a Hebrew name, but there is no proof that Peter was a descendant of the tribe of Simeon. Concerning his family, we know only that he was the son of John (John 21:15) and that he had a brother named Andrew (John 1:40). The Bible does not say whether Peter was older or younger than Andrew.

PLACES OF RESIDENCE

The first mention of Peter's residence appears in John 1:44, where we read: "Now Philip was from Bethsaida, of the city of Andrew and Peter." Bethsaida is located on the northern shore of the Sea of Galilee. Later, after the Lord called Peter into His service, Peter was residing in Capernaum with Andrew (Mark 1:21, 29).

EDUCATION

The New Testament does not give specific details regarding Peter's formal education. However, we read in Acts 4:13 that the religious leaders were amazed at the confidence of Peter and John because they were "uneducated and untrained men." From this, some have concluded that Peter had not received any kind of formal schooling. Such a conclusion misrepresents the statement of the religious leaders and discredits Peter. The real implication of this statement is that Peter and John were unschooled in rabbinical lore, and the religious leaders marveled that Peter and John, being laymen, understood the meaning of the Scriptures they quoted. Peter undoubtedly had received the elementary education given Jewish boys of that day.

OCCUPATION

Like many others reared in a fishing village on the Sea of Galilee, Peter and his brother Andrew were fishermen by trade. Since a boy usually learned the trade of his father, it is reasonable to conclude that Peter's father was also a fisherman. Peter and Andrew were partners in their business enterprise with a man

named Zebedee and his sons, James and John. The fact that Peter's
father is not mentioned in connection with the business may imply
that he was deceased (see Luke 5:7; cf. Mark 1:20). Apparently the
business was very lucrative since Peter's home in Capernaum was
large, accommodating at one time not only his immediate family,
but also the Lord and the other disciples (Mark 1:29–34).

MARITAL STATUS

Although very little is known concerning the marital status
of the rest of the disciples, there are several references to Peter
being married. One of the early miracles of Jesus was the healing of Peter's mother-in-law (Mark 1:29–31). We know that his
wife traveled with him in his ministry (1 Cor. 9:5; note that
Cephas is the Aramaic form of the name "Peter"). It is possible
that she was with Peter in "Babylon" when he wrote 1 Peter.
The Greek text simply says, "she at Babylon" (1 Peter 5:13)
and probably refers to Peter's wife, who was also sending her
greeting.

HIS CALL TO SERVICE

IN BETHANY

When John the Baptist pointed his disciples to Jesus, the one
named Andrew immediately went to find his brother Simon.
When Jesus met Simon, He said, "You are Simon the son of
John; you shall be called Cephas" (John 1:42). The writer of the
fourth gospel added the explanatory note that Cephas is translated Peter, which means in Greek *a stone* (from *petros*). Jesus,
no doubt, was giving Simon a descriptive title, but the title of
"stone" became his personal name. He is the only individual in
the New Testament called by this name.

IN CAPERNAUM

While John 1 records the first meeting of the Lord Jesus Christ
and Peter, it is doubtful that Peter and the others mentioned

there became His constant companions immediately. They apparently went back to their fishing for a period of time. Later, when the Lord began His ministry in Capernaum, He enlisted His disciples on a permanent basis. We read: "When they had brought their boats to land, they left everything and followed Him" (Luke 5:11; see also Matt. 4:18–22; Mark 1:16–20).

HIS SERVICE UNDER JESUS CHRIST

THE RANKING OF THE DISCIPLES

Whenever the disciples are listed in the New Testament, Simon Peter's name always appears first (Matt. 10:2–4; Mark 3:16–19; Luke 6:13–16; Acts 1:13). Some reason that this is because Peter was one of the first chosen to follow the Lord. Others believe Peter's natural aggressiveness marked him out as the leader of the disciples. Peter often spoke on behalf of the disciples, and the Lord occasionally addressed Peter as representing the entire body of disciples. The disciples, however, never conceded the place of leadership to Peter, as evidenced by their continual arguments about greatness (Matt. 20:20–28; Mark 9:33–34; Luke 22:24–27). While Peter's name appears first in every list, it is clear that the Lord Jesus was the leader of the disciples, each of whom had equally important responsibilities to fulfill.

THE INNER CIRCLE

Among Jesus' disciples, Peter, James, and John enjoyed a unique position, which has resulted in their being referred to as "the inner circle." The New Testament does not explain why the Lord permitted only these disciples to share three special experiences. Perhaps it was related to their future ministries.

The first special experience that these three disciples witnessed was the restoration of the daughter of Jairus back to life (Mark 5:37–43; Luke 8:51–56). Only her mother, her father, Peter, James, and John were permitted to view the actual miracle.

The second event took place on the Mount of Transfiguration when Jesus talked with Moses and Elijah concerning His coming death (Matt. 17:1–9; Mark 9:2–9; Luke 9:28–36). Peter was correct in understanding that this event foreshadowed the kingdom of Jesus Christ on earth, and he wanted to enter it immediately. Peter was wrong, however, in his expectation that the kingdom would be established at once.

The third event witnessed by these three took place in the Garden of Gethsemane (Matt. 26:37–46; Mark 14:33–42). There they saw the agony of our Lord as He talked with His heavenly Father concerning the trials before Him. These events undoubtedly made indelible impressions on Peter's mind and affected his later ministry.

THE GREAT TESTIMONY

Peter made a key statement in response to a question from Jesus: "Who do people say that the Son of man is?" (Matt. 16:13). Various disciples answered, "John the Baptist . . . Elijah . . . Jeremiah, or one of the prophets." The Lord's next question was, "But who do you say that I am?" It was Peter who answered, "You are the Christ, the Son of the living God" (vv. 14–16), thereby demonstrating divinely given insight. Most people believed that the Messiah would be a man elevated to the office of Messiah, but Peter's answer revealed that he believed Jesus was the Messiah and the Son of God.

The Lord's response to Peter's confession has been the subject of great debate throughout church history. It is the author's opinion that Peter is *not* the rock on which the church was to be built. Peter, as well as the other apostles, was one of the foundation stones (Eph. 2:20), but the Christ, as professed by Peter in Matthew 16, is *the* rock (the *petra* in the Greek) on which the church has been built. That Peter (*petros* in the Greek) never considered himself to be the rock, is clear from 1 Peter 2:4–8.

The nature of the "keys" that were given to Peter (Matt. 16:19) has also been the subject of much debate. The "keys" were probably symbols of authority that the apostles possessed relating to the proclamation of the gospel of Jesus Christ. Peter did not have exclusive possession of this authority (see Matt. 18:18 and John 20:23); rather it was possessed by the entire apostolic band. Peter clearly used his authority in opening the Gospel to the Jews on the day of Pentecost (Acts 2), to the people of Samaria (Acts 8), and to Gentile believers (Acts 10–11).

THE GREAT STUMBLING BLOCK

Shortly after Peter had made the greatest statement in his life, he clearly revealed his fallibility. Matthew 16:21 relates that Jesus began to tell the disciples that He must go to Jerusalem, be killed, and then be raised on the third day. It seems that Peter heard only that Jesus must be killed. Mathew tells us that Peter took the Lord aside and began to rebuke Him saying, "God forbid it, Lord! This shall never happen to You" (v. 22). Peter tried to persuade Jesus from His announced path of suffering and death. The Lord, however, saw in Peter's action Satan working to keep Him from the cross. He rebuked Peter with the sharp retort, "Get behind Me, Satan! You are a stumbling block to Me" (v. 23).

HIS ACTIVITIES DURING PASSION WEEK

OPENING EVENTS

The Scriptures do not record that Peter was involved in the early events of Passion Week, but it is quite probable he and other disciples were present when Jesus rode into Jerusalem on the colt, when many of them recognized His entry to be the fulfillment of Messianic prophecies in Zechariah 9:9 and Psalm 118:26 (see Luke 19:37–38). They probably saw Him cleanse the temple and listened to Him debate with the Jewish leaders.

THE PASSOVER FEAST

The Lord visited Jerusalem in order to celebrate the Passover feast. According to Luke 22:8, He sent Peter and John to make preparations for the observances of the Passover. This meant finding the Upper Room where the meal would take place, securing the proper sacrifice, offering the sacrifice in the temple, and preparing the meal for the evening. At dinner, Jesus began to wash the feet of the disciples (John 13:2–20), which was the task of the host. Peter objected, for he felt it was not fitting for him to be served in this way by his Lord. Jesus performed this symbolic act to show the necessity for daily cleansing from sin for the child of God. The Lord told Peter that unless He washed his feet, Peter could not share His blessing. Peter then asked the Lord to wash his hands and head also. But the Lord patiently reminded Peter that he had already bathed and therefore he needed only to wash his feet. The child of God receives a complete "bath" when he comes to know Christ as his Savior. Therefore, he does not need another "bath" when he sins. He needs only to "wash his feet," that is, to confess his sin and receive forgiveness (cf. 1 John 1:9).

During the Passover feast, it was Peter who prompted John to ask the Lord who would betray Him (John 13:24), and the Lord predicted that Peter would deny Him three times before the cock would crow (John 13:38).

THE GARDEN AND TRIALS

From the Upper Room, the disciples (including Peter) went with Jesus to Gethsemane, where they were privileged to see Him in prayer. When the Roman soldiers, accompanied by Judas, came to arrest the Lord, Peter stepped forward and drew his sword in Christ's defense (John 18:10). He cut off the ear of Malchus, a servant of the high priest, but the Lord stopped him, touched the ear, and healed the man (Luke 22:51).

When the other disciples fled into the night, Peter and "another disciple" (probably John; [John 18:15]) followed his Master from a distance. Later, as he sat around a campfire, Peter was identified as an associate of the Lord. As had been predicted, Peter then denied Jesus three times. As He was being led from one trial to another, Jesus turned and looked at Peter (Luke 22:61). When Peter met his Master's gaze, he was filled with remorse and went out and wept bitterly in deep repentance over his sin.

THE MORNING OF THE RESURRECTION

We do not know whether Peter witnessed the crucifixion of the Lord, for the Scripture is silent on that fact. But we do know he was in Jerusalem on the morning of the Resurrection, since the angel that appeared to the women instructed them to tell Peter that Jesus had arisen (Mark 16:7). When Peter heard the news, he ran with John to the tomb. Peter was the first disciple to enter the tomb and see the grave clothes (John 20:2–8). It has been assumed by many that the Lord appeared to Peter on the day of His resurrection. According to Paul, He appeared to Peter after the Resurrection, before He appeared to the Twelve (1 Cor. 15:5).

HIS MOVEMENT FROM CHRIST'S RESURRECTION TO THE ASCENSION

FISHING IN GALILEE

Some time after the Resurrection, Peter said, "I am going fishing" (John 21:3). In Galilee he was met by the Lord, who gave him a threefold commission to serve Him (John 21:15–23). Following this meeting, Peter returned to Jerusalem.

WAITING IN JERUSALEM

At His last appearance to the disciples, Jesus commanded them to wait in Jerusalem for the baptism of the Holy Spirit (Acts 1:4–5). Peter and the others were privileged to see Him ascend into heaven and heard the promise from the angel that the Lord would return to earth just as He had gone into heaven (Acts 1:11).

While the disciples were waiting, as they had been commanded, Peter urged his brethren to select someone to fill the position vacated by Judas. He pointed out that Judas' denial of the Lord was a fulfillment of prophecy (Acts 1:15–22). Some expositors have criticized Peter's actions, saying that Paul, not Matthias, was the twelfth apostle. Yet, the term "the Twelve" had become a common designation for the disciples, and it must have been a source of great embarrassment that the Twelve had become eleven. Possibly their opponents made fun of the disciples, emphasizing that there had been a traitor within their ranks. Perhaps Peter wanted to squelch such criticism and make "the Twelve" really twelve again.

HIS MINISTRY IN THE CHURCH

ON THE DAY OF PENTECOST

When the Holy Spirit came upon the disciples on the Day of Pentecost, the disciples began to speak in the languages of the Jews who were gathered from all over the Roman Empire to celebrate the feast (Acts 2:4–11). It was Peter, however, who stood up to deliver what could be called the main address of the day. The theme of his message to the nation of Israel was that Jesus of Nazareth, whom they had crucified, is "both Lord and Christ," that is, the Messiah (Acts 2:36). The only avenue open to the nation was to repent (change their minds) concerning Jesus of Nazareth, and accept Him as their Savior (Acts 2:38–39). The power of the Holy Spirit in the life of Peter and the other disciples was evident on this occasion, for three thousand persons came to know Jesus Christ as Savior that day (Acts 2:41, 47).

IN DEVELOPMENTS IN THE CHURCH

Peter played a central role in the development of the church as recorded in the first portion of Acts. When persecution developed, it was Peter who stood to defend the action that he and the other disciples had taken (Acts 4:1–12, 19–20). When the first serious case of sin entered the church through the deception of Ananias and Sapphira, it was Peter who announced God's judgment on the couple (5:1–11). It was Peter and John who went to Samaria to check the claim that the Samaritans had received the Word of God (8:14).

In Acts 10 and 11, we read about a most significant event. Peter was shown, through a vision, that foods which had been forbidden as unclean by the Mosaic Law were now permitted. Because of this vision, Peter proclaimed the good news of Jesus Christ to the Gentile Cornelius and to his household. The Holy Spirit fell on Cornelius and his household in Caesarea, just as He had on the disciples in Jerusalem on the day of Pentecost (11:15). From this experience, Peter learned that Gentiles were to be included in the church on an equal basis with Jews.

When the question of Gentile status in the church finally came to a "showdown," Peter, along with Paul and Barnabas, were there to testify concerning the facts as they knew them (Acts 15:7–12). The Jerusalem council decided that it was unnecessary for Gentiles to become Jews in order to obtain salvation in Jesus Christ.

HIS FINAL YEARS AND DEATH

After Peter's miraculous deliverance from prison, "he left and went to another place" (Acts 12:17). Exactly where he went has been the subject of speculation throughout church history. Except for his participation in the Jerusalem council (Acts 15), there are no further references in the book of Acts to Peter or his ministry.

Paul mentioned Peter and his travels with his wife in the first letter to the Corinthians (9:5). Galatians 2:7–9 states that Peter carried on a ministry mainly to Jewish believers. He did not minister to Jewish brethren exclusively, however, for Paul noted in this same passage that Peter was guilty of inconsistent conduct (Gal. 2:11–14). Peter apparently had been eating with Gentile Christians and enjoying their fellowship. When Jewish brethren came from James, he refrained from eating with the Gentile Christians and thereby caused a rift. Paul said that he opposed Peter to his face because he was acting wrongly toward the Gentile believers.

Peter probably did not spend much time in Rome. It is

doubtful that he was in Rome before Paul wrote his letter to the Romans. Had Peter been there, surely Paul would have known it and greeted him by name. Many believe that Peter went to Rome about the time of Paul's release from his first Roman imprisonment (about A.D. 62). Whether 1 Peter was actually written from Babylon on the Euphrates River (1 Peter 5:13), or whether Peter was in Rome using the term "Babylon" symbolically has been debated for centuries. (See further discussion in chapter 2.)

Tradition states that Peter was crucified in Rome during the persecutions of Nero sometime late in A.D. 67 or early in A.D. 68, when he was approximately seventy-five years old. Though there is little evidence to support the tradition that he was crucified upside down, this may, in fact, have been the case.

SOME REVIEW QUESTIONS

1. What biographical facts are found in Scripture concerning the man named Peter?

2. When did Peter's relationship with Jesus Christ begin and what special privilege did he have as one of Jesus' disciples?

3. What was the significant testimony that Peter gave concerning the person of Jesus? Did that make Peter "the rock" on which the church has been built?

4. What was Peter's role in the early development of the church? How was he involved in the spread of the Gospel to the Gentiles?

5. What do we know biblically of Peter's final years? According to church tradition, how and when did he die?

2
PETER THE AUTHOR

In chapter 1, we noted that the religious leaders knew Peter and John to be "uneducated and untrained men" (Acts 4:13). Though some have thereby concluded that Peter could not have written the two letters bearing his name, Peter was "uneducated and untrained" simply in regard to formal Jewish studies. No doubt he had an elementary education; that Peter knew how to read and to write can hardly be debated. Although Peter's native tongue was not Greek, there is no reason to deny that he could speak and write it.

The other New Testament writers, many of whom also came from Galilee, knew Greek. James, who probably never left Palestine, wrote very acceptable Greek in the epistle that bears his name. John Mark's home was Jerusalem, the stronghold of the Aramaic language, yet Mark wrote in very fine Greek. Should not Peter also have been able to do this? Undoubtedly Peter's travels throughout the Greek-speaking world improved his ability to communicate in this language. On a number of occasions, he probably had to preach publicly in Greek.

The case for Peter having a good knowledge of Greek is buttressed by the fact that his two letters were written near the close of his life; thus he would have been using the language a long time.

THE AUTHORSHIP OF 1 AND 2 PETER

While those who are conservative in their theological thinking accept the fact that Peter wrote both New Testament books
that bear his name, not everyone shares that conclusion. Some
question whether 2 Peter, in particular, was actually written by
Peter. They believe that 2 Peter should not be included in the list
of books regarded by the church as inspired Scripture.

How can we know which books should be included in the
Bible? Over the centuries, men led by the Holy Spirit have determined which books bore the marks of inspiration. Some of the
questions that the early church fathers seemed to have used in
attempting to recognize the canonical works were:

1. Is the book written or backed by a known apostle?

2. Does the book come with divine authority, clearly reflecting
   a "Thus says the Lord" approach?

3. Does the book's content measure up with the remainder of
   accepted Scripture? (Many books were rejected because of this
   test.)

4. Does the book give evidence of divine inspiration? By "divine
   inspiration" was meant, Had it demonstrated the power of
   God in the lives of the believers, and could it substantiate its
   claims?

5. Is the book widely accepted by God's people?

Although these five questions are not formally written down
anywhere, they apparently were applied to the various writings
to determine which books should be included in the New Testament canon. The word *canon* comes from a Greek word, which
is probably a derivative of a Hebrew word meaning a reed, or a
measuring rod. The Hebrew term is used this way in Ezekiel
40:3 and 42:16. The church never officially placed any book
into the New Testament canon that it later removed. We must
understand that the church did not make the books inspired.

They were simply recognizing and acknowledging the *inherent* inspiration of the books, that is, the authenticity and authority of them. Although different church fathers as early as the second century acknowledged various New Testament books as inspired Scripture, the first official listing of a New Testament canon occurred at the Third Council of Carthage in A.D. 397.

In support of the view that both 1 and 2 Peter belong in the sacred canon, we will first examine the evidence that comes to us from outside the Bible. This is called the external evidence. Later we will examine the evidence within the books, which is called the internal evidence.

External Evidence for Authenticity

1 PETER. External evidence from church history supports the argument that this book was written by Peter. No other book in the whole New Testament canon has earlier or stronger attestation than 1 Peter. Church fathers such as Polycarp[1] and Clement of Rome[2] quoted from the work in their own letters, although they did not name Peter as the source of their quotations. It was common practice to quote from a work without mentioning the author. The first church father to mention Peter as the author was Irenaeus.[3] Eusebius[4] included 1 Peter in the class of books that was acknowledged by the entire church as canonical. The external evidence (of which only a small portion has been given here) for Peter being the author of 1 Peter is indeed strong.

2 PETER. While the external evidence for 1 Peter is very strong, the case with 2 Peter is exactly the opposite. Second Peter is quoted in the works of church fathers such as Justin Martyr,[5] Irenaeus, Ignatius,[6] and Clement of Rome, but none of them mentions Peter as the source of the quotations used. The fact that they quoted from the book shows that they considered it to be of great value. When one considers the brevity of the second letter, it is significant that all these men would quote it. The first man to connect the name of Peter with 2 Peter was Origen (about A.D. 250), and he acknowledged that the book's authenticity was disputed. Eusebius had some doubts concerning its authenticity, although he acknowledged that many individuals

did accept the work as genuine. The Third Council of Carthage (A.D. 397) recognized the book as genuine and declared it to be part of the canon.

There are reasons why the external evidence for 2 Peter is very meager. Owing to the very nature and brevity of the letter, there are few quotable phrases in it. It is also possible that this letter did not circulate widely and for this reason might have been regarded with suspicion. Since the content of the letter strongly opposes false teachers, undoubtedly they would have made every effort to discredit and suppress the book. The important thing is that the epistle was recognized as authentic from at least the fourth century.

INTERNAL EVIDENCE FOR AUTHENTICITY

1 PETER. The evidence found within the book supports the apostle Peter as the author. In verse 1 of chapter 1, the author identifies himself as "Peter, an apostle of Jesus Christ." As we pointed out in the last chapter, only one man in the entire New Testament is known by the name of Peter.

Further internal evidence that Peter wrote this epistle lies in several allusions to the ministry of the Lord. In 1 Peter 5:2, the author admonishes the elders to "shepherd the flock of God among you." These are practically the same words that Jesus spoke to Peter (John 21:15-17). In 1 Peter 5:5, the writer urges all believers to "clothe yourselves with humility toward one another." An example of humility is found in John 13:2-17, where we learn that the Lord clothed Himself with humility by girding Himself with a towel and washing the disciples' feet. A third allusion to the ministry of the Lord is found in 1 Peter 5:7, where the author writes, "casting all your anxiety on Him, because He cares for you"; compare the Lord's statement in Matthew 11:28-30. There is also a genuine similarity between this letter and the speeches of Peter contained in the book of Acts. Compare the following passages:

1 PETER	ACTS
1:17	10:34–35
1:21	2:32–36; 10:40–41
2:7–8	4:10–11
2:24	5:30; 10:39

The evidence within the epistle of 1 Peter strongly argues that the apostle Peter is the author.

2 PETER. Although the external evidence for 2 Peter is not strong, the internal evidence argues strongly that the apostle Peter wrote it. The author calls himself "Simon Peter, a bond-servant and apostle of Jesus Christ" (1:1).

Some contend that the opening itself demonstrates that 2 Peter is a forgery, since Peter uses both names in introducing himself, in contrast to the introduction of 1 Peter. On the contrary, the addition of the name Simon argues strongly for the fact that Peter is the author. Think for a minute about how a forger works. If you lived in the second century and wanted to write a book that everyone would think was written by Peter, how would you start? Would you not go to the known writings of Peter (1 Peter) and begin your letter in exactly the same way? A forger copies things exactly as they are. He never makes changes. Peter, however, would have felt free to begin his letter any way he wanted. Do you always sign your name exactly the same way on all letters? Probably not, and neither did Peter.

Some experiences mentioned in the second letter also correspond to two specific events in Peter's life—the Transfiguration, and the prophecy of Peter's death. The Transfiguration is mentioned in 2 Peter 1:16–18 (see Matt. 17:1–9; Mark 9:2–9; Luke 9:28–36). Peter felt free to quote only that portion of the speech of the voice from heaven that fit his purpose. He left out the words, "listen to Him!" Would a second century forger have taken such liberties with the texts of the known gospels? The second event from Peter's life is reflected in 2 Peter 1:13–15. Peter anticipated that he was about to die as the Lord Jesus had revealed. This naturally brings to mind the account in John 21:18–19, for

Jesus had told Peter that he would die in old age.

A reference to a previous epistle is contained in 2 Peter 3:1. This argues that Peter is the author of both epistles. Finally, we note that there are many similarities between 1 and 2 Peter in subject matter. For example:

SUBJECT MATTER	1 PETER	2 PETER
1. Eschatology [study of last things]	1:5	3:7
2. Prophecy	1:10–12	1:19–21; 3:2
3. The Flood	3:20	2:5; 3:5–6
3. Liberty	2:16	2:19

Therefore, we see that the internal evidence of 2 Peter does support Peter as the author of the epistle.

Why have the critics attacked 2 Peter so severely? One reason is that the writer seems to have borrowed from the book of Jude. A comparison of 2 Peter and the book of Jude reveals that there are similarities between these two books. Peter and Jude use two of the same Old Testament illustrations of judgment. However, each uses a third example which the other does not mention.

2 PETER 2:4–9	JUDE VV. 5–7
The angels that sinned	The children of Israel in the wilderness
The old world before the flood	The angels that sinned
Sodom and Gomorrah	Sodom and Gomorrah

Furthermore, there are other differences in the two books. Second Peter seems to anticipate that false teachers will come, while Jude states that they are already present. Of the two epistles, Jude is probably the later one, and if either borrowed from the other, Jude was probably the borrower.

A second objection is raised over the differences in style

between 1 and 2 Peter in the language of the original Greek text. But that does not prove Peter could not have written both letters. The difference may be attributed to the use of a secretary. Peter stated in the first letter (5:12) that he wrote through Silvanus, but he made no such statement concerning a secretary in the second letter.

Finally, some critics have objected to the Petrine authorship of 2 Peter on the grounds that the writer was too eager to show that he was the apostle Peter. They hold that the writer brought in historical events such as the Transfiguration and the prophesied death of Jesus to convince the readers that Peter wrote the epistle. The only answer to this objection is that there is no answer. If the author had not mentioned any personal facts, the critics would have rejected the book because no personal events were included. A hostile critic can never be satisfied.

THE ADDRESSEES OF 1 AND 2 PETER

It is stated in 2 Peter 3:1 that this is Peter's second letter to these "beloved" believers. Therefore, we assume both letters were directed to the same group of believers. But there is a further problem that should be discussed: To whom were the letters sent? There are three views concerning the identity of the recipients: (1) they were Jewish Christians; (2) they were Gentile Christians; (3) they were Jewish and Gentile Christians. This author believes that Peter's epistles were directed to the last group, but we will examine the evidence for each of the theories.

THE ADDRESSEES ARE JEWISH CHRISTIANS

Some expositors of the Scriptures believe that only Jewish believers were addressed in these letters. First, they point out Galatians 2:7–8, which says Peter was the apostle to the circumcision and Paul the apostle to the Gentiles. Second, 1 Peter 1:1 refers to "those who reside as aliens, scattered throughout Pontus, Galatia, Cappadocia, Asia, and Bithynia." In the Greek text, the word used for "aliens" is a term referring to Jews who lived in the *Diaspora,* that is, outside Jerusalem. Third, there are many quotations and allusions to the Old Testament. These three points have led some to the conclusion that Peter directed his letters toward Jewish Christians who had been scattered from Jerusalem into the region of what is known today as Turkey.

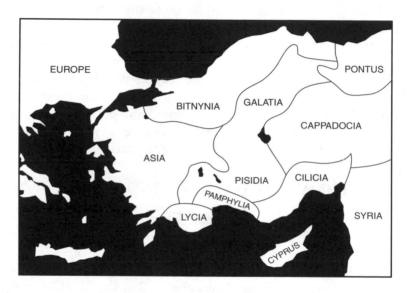

THE ADDRESSEES ARE GENTILE CHRISTIANS

Some expositors believe that Peter's letters were addressed to the Gentile Christians whom he had met in his travels. Those who hold this position point out, first, that Peter used the term "aliens" (1 Peter 1:1) to mean that these Christians were dispersed into the earth from their real home, which is heaven (cf. 1 Peter 2:11). Second, they point out that in 1 Peter 1:14, Peter refers to former times of "ignorance." It is usually not thought that Jews were ever in ignorance when it came to spiritual issues, but that could be said about Gentiles (see Eph. 4:17–19). In the same vein, 1 Peter 4:3–5 refers to former times of "abominable idolatries." It could not have been said that the Jews were idolaters, but Gentiles were often called idolaters. Therefore, some believe that Peter's readers were Gentiles.

THE ADDRESSEES ARE JEWISH AND GENTILE CHRISTIANS

It is more likely that the epistles of 1 and 2 Peter were addressed to both Jewish and Gentile Christians. The fact that Peter was the apostle to the Jews and Paul to the Gentiles (Gal. 2:7–8) defines the primary ministry of each man. However, there was some overlap in their ministries. In the passage that follows the statement in Galatians 2, Paul took Peter to task for his actions toward the Gentile Christians. Peter was obviously ministering to these Gentile Christians in some way. Paul, the apostle to the Gentiles, customarily went to the synagogue first, whenever he entered a new town (cf. Acts 13:5, 14; 14:1; 17:1–2, 10, 16–17; 18:4, etc.). The term "aliens" may refer to Jewish brethren or to Gentiles in the sense of 1 Peter 2:11, those displaced from their heavenly home. The times of ignorance and idolatry (1 Peter 1:14; 4:3–5) could be directed at Gentiles, and the Old Testament quotations and allusions would appeal to the Jewish brethren.

Since the churches to which the letters were sent included both Jews and Gentiles, we may conclude that Peter did not address either group exclusively. Rather, he addressed Christians, whatever their national origin.

THE OCCASION AND PURPOSE OF 1 AND 2 PETER

PERSECUTIONS

At the time when 1 and 2 Peter were written, Christianity was beginning to be considered a religious entity separate from Judaism. Consequently Christians no longer had the protection accorded those adhering to the official religion and were coming under persecutions from the state. In the first epistle, one gets the impression that these persecutions were just beginning and were primarily on a local level. Although suffering religious persecution was nothing new for the Jews, it was new for the Gentile Christians.

EXHORTATIONS

In light of the persecutions the believers were experiencing, Peter determined to write to exhort them concerning God's grace in their lives (1 Peter 5:12). As time passed, however, it became obvious that a far greater problem was developing within the churches. Between the writing of his first and second letters, Peter became aware of the fact that false teachers were beginning to creep into the congregations, and he knew that great difficulties would follow. He wrote the second letter, therefore, to warn the believers against the false teachers who would enter the flock (2 Peter 3:17–18). He also urges the believers to "grow in the grace and knowledge of our Lord and Savior Jesus Christ."

THE PLACE OF WRITING

1 PETER. First Peter was written from "Babylon" (5:13). The identity of Babylon has been debated among Bible expositors for centuries. Three views have developed as possible explanations.

The first view is that Peter used the term *Babylon* to conceal his true location, which was in Rome. Some argue that Rome was not known by the term *Babylon* until John late in the first century wrote the book of Revelation. There is some evidence, however, that the metaphor was used even before the days of Peter. Rome was a luxurious city given over to the worship of false gods much like Babylon, and perhaps it came to be known as "Babylon" in Christian circles. It may be observed that the entire sentence in which the expression occurs has a figurative tone, since Mark was not the natural son of Peter (5:13). It is more probable that Mark and Silvanus would join Peter in the capital of the empire rather than some distant outpost (5:12–13). The location of the writing is a difficult issue, but evidence seems to favor the earliest tradition, that Peter was in Rome.

A second view is that Peter was writing from Babylon, the city located on the Euphrates River. This view is supported by the fact that for these readers this would have been the literal understanding of the word *Babylon*. Scholars holding this opinion say that nothing else in 1 Peter is taken as allegory; therefore, the term "Babylon" should not be taken allegorically or metaphorically to mean Rome.

A third view is that Babylon refers to a city of that name located in Egypt. This "Babylon" was a military outpost of no great significance. There is no evidence that Peter was ever in Egypt, although the Coptic (North African) Church has traditionally accepted this location for the writing of 1 Peter. It seems highly improbable that we would find Peter, Mark, and Silvanus together at such a remote outpost. After examining the various possibilities concerning the location from which 1 Peter was written, this author concludes that it was probably written in Rome.

2 PETER. Although Peter does not name the location from which he wrote his second letter, it was probably written from Rome also. Peter wrote that he expected to die shortly, and tradition says that he was crucified in Rome. It is reasonable to conclude that the letter was written from Rome.

THE DATE OF WRITING

1 PETER. Since 1 Peter was written with reference to persecutions, the letter is usually dated by the persecutions of Nero, which began in A.D. 64. A conservative estimate of early A.D. 65 is probably close to the actual date of composition.

2 PETER. The traditional date for the death of Peter is late A.D. 67 or early A.D. 68. Since this letter was written shortly before his death (1:13–15), we may date this epistle as late A.D. 67.

SOME OUTSTANDING CHARACTERISTICS
OF 1 AND 2 PETER

1 PETER

There are several notable qualities of these two letters by Peter the apostle. First, the initial epistle bears a striking similarity to the writings of the apostle Paul:

1 PETER	PAUL'S WRITINGS
1:3	Ephesians 1:3
1:14	Ephesians 2:3
1:21	Romans 4:23–24
2:18	Ephesians 6:5
3:1	Ephesians 5:22
5:10–11	Philippians 4:19–20

Second, the illustration in 1 Peter 3:18–22 is one of the most misunderstood passages in the Bible, leading to questions about a second chance and baptism for salvation.

Third, the book emphasizes the sufferings of Christ (1:11, 19–21; 2:21–24; 3:18; 4:13; 5:1) and the return of the Lord (1:3, 13, 21; 3:15).

Fourth, the book includes many quotations from and allusions to the Old Testament.

2 PETER

First, this epistle is written in a graphic style with lively descriptions: 1:9, 13–14; 2:3, 8; 3:10, 16.

Second, there is a great similarity between 2 Peter 2 and the book of Jude.

Third, the epistle contains a great number of words in the original Greek (fifty-four) which occur only once in the entire Bible. (Any Greek word that only appears once in the text of the Scripture is called a *hapax legomena* by Greek Bible scholars.)

SOME REVIEW QUESTIONS

1. Which of the two letters written by Peter has stronger evidence to support its authorship?

2. How would you support the Petrine authorship of both 1 and 2 Peter from an internal and an external standpoint?

3. It is thought that both 1 and 2 Peter went to the same groups of people, but what was the basic makeup of the recipients?

4. Why do you think Peter wrote the two letters that bear his name?

5. From what location do you believe Peter wrote his two letters?

NOTES

1. Polycarp (ca. A.D. 70–155) was the bishop of Smyrna and wrote a letter to the church in Philippi. He was martyred.

2. Clement (ca. A.D. 30–100) was an elder in the church in Rome and wrote a letter to the church in Corinth.

3. Irenaeus (ca. A.D. 104–203) was the bishop of Smyrna, who exposed various types of Gnostic heresies.

4. Eusebius (ca. A.D. 265–340), a bishop of Caesarea, has been called the father of church history.

5. Justin Martyr (ca. A.D. 100–165) started a Christian school in Rome where he was later martyred.

6. Ignatius (unknown—ca. A.D. 107), a bishop of Antioch in Syria, wrote letters to churches he visited on his way to Rome to be martyred.

FIRST PETER

OUTLINE OF FIRST PETER

I. INTRODUCTION (1:1–2)
   A. The author (1:1a)
   B. The addressees (1:1b–2)

II. CANTICLE OF PRAISE (1:3–12)
   A. The new birth (1:3b)
   B. The living hope (1:3c)
   C. The glorious inheritance (1:4)
   D. The omnipotent Protector (1:5–12)

III. CONDUCT BEFORE GOD (1:13–2:12)
   A. Holiness (1:13–16)
   B. Love (1:17–25)
   C. Growth (2:1–8)
   D. Praise (2:9–12)

IV. CONDUCT BEFORE MEN (2:13–4:19)
   A. The Christian and his government (2:13–17)
   B. The Christian and his business (2:18–25)
   C. The Christian and his family (3:1–7)
   D. The Christian and his society (3:8–22)
   E. The Christian and Christ's example (4:1–19)

V. CONDUCT IN THE CHURCH (5:1–11)
   A. Conduct of the pastor (5:1–4)
   B. Conduct of the people (5:5–11)

VI. CONCLUSION (5:12–14)

SOURCE: Adapted from Elvis E. Cochrane, *The Epistles of Peter* (Grand Rapids: Baker, 1965). Used by permission.

3

A CANTICLE OF PRAISE

The first section of 1 Peter (1:1–12) forms the foundation for the entire book. In this section, the apostle Peter expresses thanksgiving for the eternal salvation that God offers to every individual. His words form a song, or canticle, of praise to the Creator. An understanding of these verses is essential to our comprehension of the entire epistle.

INTRODUCTION (1:1–2)

THE AUTHOR (1:1*a*)

Peter uses a common introduction to begin his epistle. He states his position as "an apostle of Jesus Christ," that is, one sent to serve and proclaim Him. This commission gave Peter the authority to write this letter to the Christian community.

The background of the apostle Peter himself has already been discussed. (See the discussions in chapters 1 and 2.) Remember that the name Peter (*Cephas* in Aramaic) was the nickname that the Lord gave Simon when they first met (John 1:42). Peter was truly a "rock" in the first century church.

THE ADDRESSEES (1:1*a*–2)

The literal meaning of the Greek text is not clearly brought over in the *New American Standard Bible* (nor other translations), which refers "to "those who reside as aliens, scattered throughout." Peter was writing his epistle literally to "the elect," those who were sojourners of the dispersion." With the term "elect," Peter indicates the relationship of his readers to God, for election carries the idea of being "chosen" by God to be His sons. He also emphasizes their relationship to the world. In Peter's view, his readers were sojourners, that is people scattered throughout a specific region. In his thinking, heaven is the real home of the Christian, and he is in this world only temporarily.

Peter directed this letter specifically to Christians scattered in the region of modern-day Turkey. Five Roman provinces are mentioned: Pontus, Galatia, Cappadocia, Asia, and Bithynia. It was Peter's intention that his letter should circulate among brethren in these provinces (see map on page 32).

In verse 2, Peter explains the use of the term "elect" or "chosen." He discusses the part each member of the Godhead plays in the salvation of an individual. First, election is "according to the foreknowledge" of *God the Father.* In other words, election began in the Father's original plan or purpose. Sanctification, which carries the idea of being "set apart" or "being made holy," is the part played by the *Holy Spirit:* "by the sanctifying work of the Spirit." It is the Holy Spirit who conforms the individual to the image of Jesus Christ through spiritual growth (2 Cor. 3:18).

In this verse, the third member of the Trinity named is *Jesus Christ,* who shed His blood and died as a sacrifice so that man might enter into this blessed relationship with God. In the life of each individual there must be obedience to the ministry of the Holy Spirit in order to experience the sanctification which God has ordained.

In this letter, it is clear that Peter is addressing true believers. To these believers, he sends "grace and peace," which may be understood as Peter's prayer for them. Peter may have included this with the thought that these two virtues would equip them to face the persecutions that might come their way.

CANTICLE OF PRAISE (1:3–12)

THE NEW BIRTH (1:3*b*)

Peter begins his song of praise to God with the words, "Blessed be the God and Father of our Lord Jesus Christ." This phrase was commonly used in ascriptions of praise to God. It is a distinctively Christian blessing. Only the Christian blesses God as the Father of the incarnate Son and as the One who raised Jesus from the dead (v. 3*c*). Here Peter makes a complete statement regarding the deity and the humanity of Jesus Christ. He emphasizes that Jesus is both Lord and Christ, which affirms His deity. And he calls Him "our" Jesus, which emphasizes the fact that Jesus Christ was a human being.

The praise that Peter expresses in the beginning of verse 3 is in response to what God has done for man: "according to His great mercy [He] has caused us to be born again." The child of God has entered into the family of God through the new birth. This salvation comes from the mercy of God, a mercy which is most abundant. The word "mercy" is used in the New Testament to describe the kindness of God in bringing the outsider to salvation. His mercy has led to the new birth, to which verses 3 and 23 refer. (Peter probably knew of Jesus' conversation with Nicodemus, recorded in John 3:1–21.) The new birth is the act of regeneration, or the act of making new, by which the believer receives new life (cf. Titus 3:5), that is, eternal life in Jesus Christ. Peter rejoices because his readers have come into a realization of their new life in Christ, through faith in Him as the Son of God.

Pause for a moment and ask yourself this question: *Am I experiencing this new life in Christ?* Jesus Christ died on the cross so that you would not have to pay the penalty for your own sin (Rom. 6:23). But you must personally receive Him into your life in order to make His death effective to redeem you from your sin (John 1:12). If you have never done so, won't you accept God's free gift of salvation by receiving Jesus Christ as your Savior right now?

THE LIVING HOPE (1:3*c*)

The new birth brings a new hope into the life of the believer. This living hope is a result of the believer's personal relationship with the living Savior. The One to whom the believer looks for salvation lives forever, having been resurrected from the dead. The resurrection was God's final affirmation of Jesus Christ. If Jesus Christ had not actually come from God, and if He had not accomplished man's redemption on the cross, He would never have been raised from the dead. Paul makes this point very clear when he writes that Jesus Christ "was delivered over because of our transgressions, and was raised because of [or on account of] our justification" (Rom. 4:25). We, as believers, have a living hope because our hope is based in a living Savior!

THE GLORIOUS INHERITANCE (1:4)

In addition to receiving a new, living hope through the new birth, the Christian is born into the family of God. Therefore he becomes an heir to the glorious inheritance of God. It is apparent from Peter's descriptions, which are expressed in three negative Greek terms, that it is a heavenly, not an earthly, inheritance. First, our inheritance is said to be "imperishable," which carries the idea that it is not subject to decay. Second, our inheritance is "undefiled," or without any defect or flaw. Third, our inheritance "will not fade away." The choice of these three negative words in the original Greek text especially emphasizes permanence and unchangeableness. The Christian's inheritance is subject neither to external defilement nor to internal corruption.

Peter also presents a positive term to describe the believer's inheritance, for he says that our inheritance has been "reserved in heaven." It is waiting to be claimed by the heir. Meanwhile, it is kept safe in a place where no thief can steal it. When the child of God enters into his inheritance, he will be with his Lord and he will be like Him (1 John 3:2). The Holy Spirit's ministry in the life of each Christian is a little taste of what will ultimately be the possession of the Christian. The indwelling of the Holy

Spirit is the down payment on the heavenly inheritance that God makes to each believer in this life. It is the guarantee of the full inheritance to follow (Eph. 1:13–14).

THE OMNIPOTENT PROTECTOR (1:5–12)

Although the believer has a new hope and a glorious inheritance awaiting him in heaven, he does not yet possess all that is his. Nevertheless in this life, the Christian has One who guards him until that moment when he will enter into his inheritance. The One who protects the Christian is God Himself since believers are "protected by the power of God" (v. 5). Here Peter employs a Greek word, "protected," which literally means "to guard." The believer's faith and trust secures the protection of God until the time when the child of God will stand before his Father in heaven, and his ultimate salvation will be revealed. Until that day, the believer is guarded by the One who possesses *all power*—the omnipotent protector.

Although such wonderful truths will strike a note of rejoicing in the heart of the believer, the thought of persecution seems to be foremost in Peter's mind. In verses 6–12, he digresses briefly from his main theme to remind his readers that in the midst of suffering, which his readers were apparently experiencing, it is easy to forget that God watches over His children. Peter says that they might "for a little while" be "distressed by various trials" (v. 6). A form of the same word for "trials" is used in James 1:12. In both James and 1 Peter, the emphasis seems to be on the sufferings that arise from external causes, not from sources within the individual.

Peter declares such temptations are a "proof [or a proving] of your faith" (v. 7), an idea also found in James 1:3. The periods of sorrow that we as Christians experience in our lives may be to prove our faith; that is, to test, to try, and to strengthen it. Like physical muscles that must be exercised in order to be strengthened, our faith must be exercised if it is to grow strong.

In verse 7, Peter uses the illustration of the gold refining process. Fire is used to remove all the impurities in the metal. Men take great care to make gold as pure as possible, and yet it is

image of Christ

something that will one day perish. Faith, however, is of much greater value than gold, because faith is more enduring. We enter these periods of testing because God wants Christians to be fashioned into the image of His Son. One day believers will "be found to result in praise and glory and honor at the revelation of Jesus Christ" (v. 7).

The reference to the Lord Jesus reminds Peter that, even in his day, few Christians had been privileged to see the Lord (v. 8). Peter himself had been with the Lord, but those to whom he was writing had placed their faith in Someone they had never seen. This is also true of Christians today. Although we cannot see the Lord physically, nevertheless we believe in Him and rejoice. The word Peter uses for "greatly rejoice" is a word expressing deep emotion, and it also appears in verse 6. Peter is speaking of a spiritual joy that is so deep and personal that it cannot be adequately formulated in words. He says that such inexpressible joy is "full of glory," or glorified.

The child of God understands what Peter is saying. This inexpressible joy is really a little taste of heaven that God permits us to enjoy while we are still here on earth. Such joy is a reflection of the glory that will be ours in heaven. It anticipates the "outcome of [our] faith," which is "the salvation of [our] souls" (v. 9). The goal that God has in view for His children is their salvation (vv. 4–5), but we need not wait until eternity to enjoy all of it. Peter views such blessings as assurances that the individual is a true child of God. There is both a present reality and a future expectation to our salvation. *joy*

In verse 10, Peter continues discussing the subject of salvation. He writes that the Old Testament prophets made careful inquiry and search concerning this salvation that Peter is extending to his readers. The Greek word for "grace" in this passage is used in the book of Acts to refer to the extension of salvation to the Gentiles (cf. Acts 14:3; 15:11; 18:27; 20:24, 32). The prophets spoke concerning "the Spirit of Christ" (v. 11), the Messiah, who was in them. They did not produce their own testimony, but they spoke His words, and their own writing made them eager to discover more concerning its full meaning (Matt. 13:17). Thus we understand that the Old Testament prophets did not construct their prophecies through their own wisdom and intelligence. Rather, they were led by the Spirit of God. They realized the importance of what they were writing, but they did not always fully understand when all these things would come to pass. This passage clearly points out the work of the Holy Spirit in the inspiration of sacred Scripture. This ministry of the Holy Spirit is discussed also in Peter's second letter (2 Peter 1:20–21).

The Spirit, in the prophets, testified concerning both "the sufferings of Christ [Messiah] and the glories to follow" (v. 11). It is significant that both the sufferings and the glory were foretold, and it was written that the glory could not be entered into apart from the sufferings (Luke 18:31–33). The time of the fulfillment of their prophecies was not revealed to the prophets. Peter writes that those living in his day were seeing the fulfillment of these prophecies in the gospel of Jesus Christ, the promised Messiah. This Gospel had been preached by Peter, Paul, and other Christians who had ministered in that region. The Holy Spirit had performed His work in applying the Gospel to the hearts of the audience. This cooperative effort (men proclaiming the Gospel and the Holy Spirit applying it in the hearts of individuals) resulted in the salvation of many in Peter's day, and it continues to result in the salvation of people today.

First Peter 1:12 comments on the angels' interest in the salvation that believers possess in Jesus Christ. It is something into which the "angels long to look." The word Peter uses for "long to look" means "to peer into." It is the same word used in John 20:5 of John stooping to peer into Jesus' open tomb on the morning of the Resurrection. This teaches that angels have an intense interest in the work of God among men on earth although they have no part in the plan of salvation. According to Luke 15:10, there is joy in the presence of the angels when a sinner repents. Paul declared that "God has exhibited us apostles last of all, as men condemned to death; because we have become a spectacle to the world, both to angels and to men." (1 Cor. 4:9). An angel from the Lord instructed Philip to go into the region of Gaza where he met the Ethiopian eunuch (Acts 8:26).

The angels who did not participate in Satan's rebellion remained holy; therefore, they are not in need of salvation. Those who followed Satan are confirmed in a state of wickedness and cannot receive salvation (James 2:19). Only man can know the salvation that God provides through Jesus Christ. But the angels stand by and study that which takes place in the lives of men who have found God's salvation. The songwriter captured this thought beautifully when he penned these words:

Holy, holy, is what the angels sing,
And I expect to help them make the courts of heaven ring;
But when I sing redemption's story, they will fold their wings,
For angels never felt the joy, that our salvation brings.[1]

A question for thoughtful reflection by regenerated individuals: What have the angels learned recently about your salvation by observing your actions?

CONCLUSION

The first section of 1 Peter is the foundation of the entire epistle. It teaches that God offers mankind redemption through the new birth. Each person who accepts God's offer receives a living hope based in a living Savior, and a glorious inheritance, which is reserved for him in heaven. During his earthly life, the believer has One who protects him, even in the midst of suffering persecution. Truly, the believer has a great salvation.

SOME REVIEW QUESTIONS

1. What part did each member of the Godhead play in the salvation of the believer, according to Peter?

2. How would you describe the living hope of the child of God?

3. What are the descriptive terms Peter applies to the believer's glorious inheritance?

4. Do persecutions that occur in the believer's life imply that God does not have sufficient power to prevent them from occurring? Then why do they happen?

5. What did the Old Testament prophets understand about the concept of salvation? Did they understand fully everything they wrote down?

NOTE

1. Johnson Oatman Jr., "Holy Holy Is What the Angels Sing." In public domain.

4

CONDUCT BEFORE GOD

Our salvation carries with it certain responsibilities that Peter discusses in the remainder of his first letter. He begins with an examination of the Christian's responsibilities to God—the vertical relationship (1:13–2:12). Then he looks at the horizontal relationship—the believer's responsibilities to other people (2:13–4:19) including relationships in the local church (5:1–11). The following chart may clarify this concept.

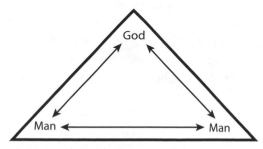

Should the working of God in salvation produce any changes in the believer? What characteristics does this new vertical relationship produce in the life of the Christian? Peter sets out to answer these questions.

HOLINESS (1:13–16)

The first word in verse 13, "Therefore," forms a bridge to all that Peter has written previously. Peter admonishes the believers to "prepare [their] minds for action." In the King James Version this expression reads vividly: "Gird up the loins of your mind." This reference would have been well understood in Peter's culture, when people wore long, flowing robes that hindered their movement. Before engaging in strenuous activity, the hem of the garment was tucked into the belt worn around the waist. This was called "girding up." Today we might use the expression "Let's roll up our sleeves." It is clear that Peter is instructing the believer to prepare his mind for serious business.

The salvation of the individual through the regenerating work of the Holy Spirit should be accompanied by a mental awakening and a new discipline of understanding. Peter urges the believer to "keep sober in spirit," an expression commonly used to signify abstinence from wine. Peter uses the expression to speak of moral alertness or sobriety. The Christian should not live a life of self-indulgence, but one of discipline and self-control, in full possession of his faculties.

Peter instructs the believer to "fix your hope completely on the grace to be brought to you at the revelation of Jesus Christ." The hope of the believer is sure, and therefore he may be confident of the Lord's favor when He appears for His own. The believer fixes his hope "completely," that is, without reservation, on the coming of the Lord. Someone has said that when the *out*look is gloomy, the believer needs to try the *up*look.

Peter urges the believer to be obedient (v. 14), not fashioning oneself according to his or her former lustful life. Christian liberty does not lead to lawlessness, but to obedience. The expression that Peter uses for "conformed" is found only twice in the New Testament—in this passage and in Romans 12:2, where it is translated, "and do not be conformed to this world." Both passages emphasize an outward pattern resulting from an inward change. The believer's life has been changed by the indwelling presence of the Holy Spirit; therefore, there should be a corresponding outward change in daily practice.

The response by the believer to the gospel of Jesus Christ has two aspects. Negatively, the child of God should not do the wicked things that were part of his or her past. Positively, the child of God should become something he was not before his conversion. Since he did not possess true knowledge previously, the purpose of his life was self-gratification. Peter teaches that the unbeliever is basically ignorant of God and His standards, whether he is a pagan Gentile or a spiritually blind Jew.

It was said that the believer should become something new. But what is that believer to become? God demands that the Christian become holy like God Himself is holy. God is completely separated from all wickedness, and the child of God should be like his heavenly Father. While the standard is clear, we must recognize that the believer is unable to attain absolute holiness in this life. He or she never loses the old nature and lives in a sinful world.

Does this mean we should throw up our hands and quit? Absolutely not! While believers cannot achieve perfect holiness in this life, they can seek to be holy in the eyes of their God. They can maintain a holy walk with the Lord. It is apparent that some Christians walk closer to the Lord than others, but the standard remains the same: the absolute holiness of the Lord Himself. Most of the problems encountered by the average Christian stem from measuring oneself by the wrong standard. The proper standard is the Lord, not some other Christian.

First Peter 1:16 contains a call to holiness that is a quotation from the book of Leviticus (see Lev. 11:44; 19:2; 20:7). God's character is absolutely holy. The Lord Jesus Christ Himself reinforced this idea in Matthew 5:48. The Christian who is related to Him should ultimately be like the One whose Name he bears.

LOVE (1:17–25)

Peter goes on to stress the love that God has shown by providing redemption for men and women at great cost. God is not a respecter of persons. He judges each individual impartially. People give great attention to superficial details such as dress and appearance, but God deals with each person according to what he or she actually is. Therefore, Peter urges us to pass the time of our stay here on earth "in fear" (v. 17), which means a healthy and holy reverence for God. The child of God does not fear Him as the heathen fear their gods. Rather, he is aware of the loving care of his heavenly Father. Life here is only a brief stay, and the believer is not to set his heart on this world.

The love of the Father is clearly demonstrated in the redemption that He has provided through the blood of Christ. The child of God has been bought out of the bondage of a vain or empty life. In the sight of God a person's life produces no worthwhile results. The price of redemption requires something beyond this transient, corrupt world—beyond silver or gold. It requires "the precious blood . . . of Christ" (v. 19). The fact that blood was shed emphasizes that His life was laid down. The blood of any man is precious to that man. But the blood of Christ is immeasurably precious, because it was shed for all mankind.

Furthermore, the shedding of the blood of Christ was the perfect sacrifice for sin. He was the "unblemished and spot-less" (v. 19) Lamb. This characterization of Christ as the Lamb of God had been made early in His ministry by John the Baptist (John 1:29, 36). But long before the time of John the Baptist, or anyone else, the work of Christ in redemption existed in the counsels of God. Before the worlds were formed, before Satan and Adam fell, before anything existed but God Himself, it was ordained that Christ would die. This fact, however, was revealed only "in these last times for the sake of you" (v. 20). While the plan was in the mind of God from all eternity, it was not made known until "the fullness of the time came" (Gal. 4:4).

God placed His stamp of approval on Jesus Christ and His death by raising Him from the dead and giving Him glory. As believers, we have a twofold reason for coming to God: (1) Christ's death and (2) His resurrection by the Father. The believer may approach God in faith knowing God will receive him because of Christ's work. One day the believer will share in Christ's glory.

The love that God has shown to the believer should prompt a response of love toward God. This love for God is demonstrated by loving fellow believers. Perhaps Peter had in mind the concept as stated in 1 John 4:20–21. Love toward God is hard to measure, but love toward the brethren is very easy to see. This is one way that we may clearly demonstrate our love for Him. Peter also says that this love ought to be a "sincere" (v. 22) love. In other words, it is not a pretense. It is to be the real thing. It must come from the heart and be demonstrated with full intensity, in an all-out manner.

Why should this be the manifestation of the Christian? Because the believer has experienced the new birth through the Word of God, which is an "imperishable" (v. 23) seed that lives and endures forever. This new life partakes of the character of a loving God. Therefore, believers should manifest love in their lives. God has demonstrated His love, and His children are to love as their heavenly Father loves. The things of this life are temporary and will ultimately fade away, but the Word of God is eternal. That eternal Word demonstrates the love of God and demands an expression of love on the part of the believer.

GROWTH (2:1–8)

As believers should demonstrate holiness of life and love in their relationship with God, so they should also be growing. We cannot manifest love toward each other unless we put away every form of antisocial evil. The word that Peter uses in 2:1 for "putting aside," is a word that carries the idea of cleansing from defilement. The things that Peter has in mind are listed in verse 1.

First on the list is "malice," which can also be translated "wickedness." This is a general term and probably refers to all kinds of evil conduct. Second, the believer should remove "all deceit" from his life. "Deceit" is a fishing word, and it literally means "to bait the hook." If you bait a hook in order to catch a fish, you are really trying to deceive the fish. He thinks a nice dinner awaits him, but he winds up getting caught on the concealed hook. The way Peter uses the word "all" in this context implies the idea of "every form of."

"Hypocrisy and envy" are apparently forms of deceit. The word *hypocrisy* comes from the Greek theatre and it carried the idea of "speaking from behind the mask." During a drama, one did not see the true emotions of the actor but only the emotion that was portrayed in the mask. *Envy* is feeling ill toward someone else's blessings.

Third, "all slander" should be removed from the life of the true child of God. Slander or evil speaking is any communication that runs down someone or attempts to belittle another person.

In verse 2, Peter takes a positive approach and urges the believer to "long for the pure milk of the word." It is through the Word that the believer is born again (cf. 1:23), and it is through the Word that the believer grows. He should desire the Word just as a newborn baby desires milk. This imagery does not demand the interpretation that the readers of this epistle were recent converts. Peter is simply saying that as a newborn desires milk, the believer ought to desire the Word of God. Those of us who have experienced the joy of giving 2:00 a.m. feedings know exactly what Peter means. Only milk satisfies the hunger within the newborn. The spiritual hunger of the believer can be satisfied only through the "milk of the word."

Do you really desire the Word of God as a newborn desires milk? Your spiritual maturity as a Christian will increase in direct proportion to the amount of time you spend studying the Word of God.

While verse 3 begins with the words "if you have tasted," the original text would permit "since you have tasted." This is the better translation. Peter is not questioning the salvation of his readers, but he is pointing out that their salvation experience is only the first "taste." The more believers feed on the Word, the more they will learn of its Author.

Peter now changes his figure of speech to that of a "living stone" (v. 4). In the remaining verses of this section, he points out that believers do not live isolated lives. They live in a community—the community of the church, in which each is joined to the others by the bond of love. As a believer partaking of the Word, the individual draws near to God with the intention of staying near and enjoying His personal fellowship. We come to

Him as unto a living stone, for indeed the Lord has been raised from the dead. While people rejected Him, God regarded Him as a very precious possession and marked Him out as such. Because of the relationship that believers have with the Lord, they, too, become living stones in a spiritual house, the church of Jesus Christ. Peter seems to be teaching something he himself once learned from his Master. When he confessed that Jesus was the Christ, the Son of God (Matt. 16:16), Jesus declared that Peter was a rock, and that he would be one of the building blocks of the church. Here in verse 5, Peter uses the same word for "built up" that the Lord used in Matthew 16:18.

Not only are believers a part of this great body of believers, but they also constitute "a holy priesthood" (v. 5). In Judaism, the priests came only from a designated tribe, that of Levi. However, in Jesus Christ, every believer is a priest, and there is no further need for a priesthood to bring men to God. Each believer may go to God directly and offer his own "spiritual sacrifices." The spiritual sacrifices we offer to God undoubtedly include the life of obedience (Rom. 12:1–2), praise, and thanksgiving to God (Heb. 13:15), and a practical ministry of doing good and sharing with all men (Heb. 13:16). These sacrifices are "acceptable to God" because they are offered through Jesus Christ.

To explain the authority for his comments, Peter turns to the prophetic Scriptures. He shows that Christ's position as the chief cornerstone of this spiritual building was foreordained by God. This idea of a foundation stone is found in several Old Testament passages (Ps. 118:22; Isa. 8:14; 28:16). Over this foundation stone, men of all ages have been divided. Those who believe in this stone have found Him to be "precious" (v. 7) and they have discovered in Him perfect peace and calmness of Spirit. This is what Peter means by the Old Testament quote, "And he who believes in Him will not be disappointed" (v. 6, from Isa. 28:16). But there are some who have rejected this stone, just as a builder preparing to construct a building discards material that is unsuitable. These who stumble over this stone will one day be judged by it. In Matthew 21:42, the Lord quoted Psalm 118:22 and applied the rejection of the stone by the builders to the Sanhedrin's conduct toward Him. Now that He has been revealed to the world, Jesus Christ stands in the way of every man and woman. Those who refuse to come to Him will be judged by Him. They refuse to accept the stone; therefore, God ordains that they shall stumble over that stone.

PRAISE (2:9–12)

Peter uses four phrases in verse 9 to describe the people of God. First, they are a "chosen race." Those who believe in Christ do not become part of Israel, but they are now the true people of God. God has chosen them for the privilege of having fellowship with Him. He chose them for obedience, that they might do His will. He chose them for service, that they might honorably serve Him.

Second, believers are "a royal priesthood." There is no separate priesthood in the church of Jesus Christ. The officers of the church are designated as "elders" and "deacons." Every believer is a priest.

Third, believers constitute "a holy nation." The word *nation* is commonly used in the plural to refer to Gentile nations, but believers constitute a distinct nation of people who are set apart, or consecrated, unto God.

Fourth, believers are "a people for God's own possession." Many of our personal possessions have no great intrinsic value, but they are valuable to us because of someone who once owned them. So it is with believers. While their personal worth is minimal, they have become increasingly valuable because of the One who possesses them.

But why has God done all these things for His children? Peter's answer is, "that you may proclaim the excellencies of Him who has called you out of darkness into His marvelous light" (v. 9). God has done all this so that the believer may proclaim the "excellencies" or the praises (virtues or qualities) of God Himself. This includes all that God is and all that He has done, as Peter states in verse 10. God has taken a group of people who were outsiders with no rights or claims to His grace, and He has included them in His program of salvation. All that God has done for the believer has been accomplished for God's glory so that He will receive the praise, not man (cf. Eph. 1:6, 12, 14).

Peter finally applies the truth of this entire section (1 Peter 1:13–2:12) to the hearts of his readers, for the believer's daily life should manifest his relationship to God. Peter admonishes us, as those who are "aliens and strangers," those who are temporary residents on this earth, to abstain from "fleshly lusts," for they war against our souls (v. 11). The term "fleshly lusts" seems to be a general term to designate all the desires that originate in man's corrupt nature. Paul talks about the same thing in Galatians 5:19–21. Peter emphasizes that the believer does not belong to this world; therefore, he ought not become part of the world around him. The real problem with fleshly lusts is that they battle against the spiritual part of the believer, that part which should grow to be holy, as our heavenly Father is holy. If the believer is to attain this holiness, he must deliberately abstain from the lusts of the world's system.

The life of the believer (v. 12) should be such that even those opposed to the believer will be forced to admit that his life commands admiration and respect. Believers in the first century were charged with many things, such as immorality, cannibalism, disloyalty to Caesar, disruption of the slave system, and breaking up homes, but their lives refuted those charges. The best arguments for Christianity are real Christians. Do our lives, including our "good deeds," commend Jesus Christ in such a way that our enemies ultimately will be forced to bring glory to God by confessing that they saw truth in our lives? May God grant that it be so!

CONCLUSION

The blessings that God has bestowed on us affect our relationship with Him. Because we are His children, we ought to be holy as the One who has called us is holy. He has demonstrated His love in providing salvation. This should stimulate in us a love for Him that is observable in our love for others. We should also continue to grow in our Christian experience through the Word. Our salvation experience is merely a "taste," and there is much more to follow. Finally, we as believers should show forth the praise of the Lord by word and deed in our daily lives, for God has accomplished a marvelous work for us who were completely undeserving.

SOME REVIEW QUESTIONS

1. If God demands holiness but believers are still sinful creatures, how can the believer ever be considered holy by God?

2. Since God loved mankind and sent His Son to redeem men and women, how can they most clearly demonstrate their love back to God?

3. Spiritual growth in the believer's life can only be accomplished when certain things are "put aside" and one thing is "longed for." What does Peter say are the things to be "put aside" and what one thing is to be "longed for"?

4. What are the privileges and responsibilities of believer-priests today?

5. What are the four descriptive phrases Peter uses to describe the people of God?

5

CONDUCT BEFORE MEN:
GOVERNMENT, BUSINESS, FAMILY

The remainder of Peter's first epistle discusses the effect our salvation should have on our relationships with our fellowmen. In the section before us, 1 Peter 2:13–3:1–7, the apostle looks at the impact our salvation should have on our relationships with those in government, business, and our family.

THE CHRISTIAN AND HIS GOVERNMENT (2:13–17)

Peter claims that the believer's salvation should always have an impact on his relationship to his government. In the final verses of the previous section (see chapter 4), Peter admonished believers to demonstrate a manner of life that will bring glory to God. One way the Christian manifests his "good deeds" (v. 12) is through submission to his government (v. 13).

Peter does not commend one form of government over another at this point. The principle is that the Christian should submit to the government under which he lives. Christianity has existed for almost two thousand years under all kinds of governmental structures. God has ordained the institution of government to provide order for society, and the Christian ought to fulfill his proper duties.

The word "submit" which Peter uses in verse 13 is a word meaning "to rank oneself under." The emphasis is on lines of delegated authority. Does this mean that the Christian is never to oppose delegated authority? The same man who wrote these words once said to a religious council, "We cannot stop speaking about what we have seen and heard" (Acts 4:20). Peter, however, felt he was in submission to authority. When arrested for preaching the gospel of Christ, he did not rebel or try to escape. Occasions may arise when the Christian feels he must obey God rather than the government, but the Christian ought to have extremely good reasons for disobeying the chosen authority. Scripture says we should submit to our government, and if we disobey, we must accept the punishment.

Submission is to be "for the Lord's sake" (v. 13). This phrase has caused some problems in interpretation. According to some, this means that the Christian should submit because the Lord Himself submitted to the authority of government. According to another interpretation, it means that our action in submitting to government will bring others to Christ. In light of the context, this second interpretation is possible. A third (and perhaps the best) explanation is that by our submission to the institution of government, which God established, we are submitting to the Lord. God ordained a chain of authoritative command in the home and the church, and we may conclude that He has ordained government to administer the affairs of the nation.

The principle of submission to government is found in many passages in the New Testament. The teaching of the Lord concerning the payment of taxes to Caesar (Matt. 22: 21), and the fact that He Himself paid taxes (Matt. 17:24–27) indicate that He submitted to the authority of government during His life on earth. When arrested, He submitted to the authority of the Roman soldiers and did not call for legions of angels to release Him (Matt. 26:52–53), even though He had committed no offense.

The apostle Paul states that the Christian should submit to the authority of government (Rom. 13:1–7) and reminds us of our responsibility to pray for those who are in positions of authority over us (1 Tim. 2:1–2). Titus 3:1–2 also confirms the principle of the authority of government.

The Old Testament enunciates the same principle. Daniel, in interpreting the dream of King Nebuchadnezzar, declared that "the God of heaven [had] given [to Nebuchadnezzar] the kingdom, the power, the strength and the glory" (Dan. 2:37). And in Daniel 4:17, the king himself would rightly acknowledge "that the living [should] know that the Most High is ruler over the realm of mankind, and bestows it on whom He wishes and sets over it the lowliest of men." The king had been removed from his throne until he learned this lesson. The Bible teaches that God is sovereign in the affairs of men, and thus we should submit to government.

Having stated the general principle of submission to the government, Peter enumerates those to whom this submission is due. He begins with the highest civil ruler of his day, the king (v. 13). However, it is not just to the head of state that the believer is to submit, but also to subordinate officials such as governors (v. 14). Since all officials receive their power from God (John 19:11), Christians are to obey them. God has established government for the well-being of the citizens, for punishment and reward. It is the will of God (v. 15) that Christians should be subject to their governments, because through their obedience, they commend themselves and their Lord. The law-abiding behavior of the believer silences those who would oppose Christ-ians and their testimony. Submission to government should be entered into freely, for the one who truly understands the commands of God will not abuse his freedom. Christians must never forget that they are "bondslaves of God" (v. 16) and ought to live as such. What rights do slaves have? Christian freedom is really the freedom to serve God, and freedom comes only as we take on the yoke of God.

Peter concludes this section on the Christian's submission to his government with a fourfold injunction which may have been a motto in the early Church: "Honor all people, love the brotherhood, fear God, honor the king" (v. 17). Remember that in Peter's day, the "king" was the Roman emperor Nero, who slandered and slaughtered Christians![1] If Peter could urge believers to submit to the authority of a ruler like Nero, surely Christians today should have no problem submitting to government officials.

THE CHRISTIAN AND HIS BUSINESS (2:18–25)

In this section, Peter mentions the Christian slave and his obligation to his master. Slavery was a way of life in the Roman Empire, and it has been estimated that there were more than sixty million slaves. They were employed in every occupation, ranging from menial manual labor to professionals, such as doctors and teachers. Peter accepted slavery as a possible social arrangement and directed Christians who find themselves in this situation to fill their place in active submission. Christians were often accused of causing difficulties between slaves and their masters. However, the teachings of the apostles never advocated rebellion on the part of the slaves.

Peter admonished Christian slaves to be subject to their masters (v. 18). This was to be their attitude, whether or not their masters were good to them. Masters were to be obeyed even if they were "unreasonable," which carries the idea of being "crooked" or a "crook." It would be easy to submit to an honorable master, but what about the one who had no concern for his slaves and was extremely difficult to please? The admonition of Peter was the same: Subject yourself to your master's authority.

Why should the servant submit? Obedience to an "unreasonable" master finds "favor" (v. 19). In the Greek text, it literally says that this is a "grace." In other words, such action is evidence of grace in the life of the individual. Perhaps Peter had in mind that such behavior is another way in which the Christian can demonstrate his "good deeds" (v. 12) before unbelievers. The servant who submits to an unreasonable or cruel master is bearing up under sorrows, but he is not enduring for the sake of sorrows. He endures because of his conscience toward God, for he is aware that God's presence is with him even in this situation. The servant who suffers for no wrongdoing follows in the steps of the Lord Jesus, who suffered undeservedly. Peter expands on the sufferings of the Lord in verses 21–25.

The proper attitude toward suffering was Peter's main concern at this point. If one is punished for doing what is wrong, he deserves it. But if the punishment that one suffers has no justification, and yet the person bears it patiently, "this finds favor with God" (v. 20).

Very few people living today are slaves. But these principles apply also to employer–employee relationships. The employee is to be submissive to his employer, even if that employer is crooked. A believer may change jobs if he has a dishonest employer. As long as he is employed by an individual or company, he should obey the directives of his employer unless they violate his responsibilities to God. Working for an "unreasonable" employer does not justify stealing time or materials from him. Obedience to one's employer, even in the smallest matters of detail, is demanded, and such obedience is a testimony to the employer.

The idea of suffering unjustly leads Peter to a brief discussion of the sufferings of our Lord (vv. 21–25). We have been called to suffer without flinching, if need be, for we see in Jesus Christ the greatest example of One who suffered unjustly without striking back. Christ left an "example for [us] to follow" (v. 21). The Greek word translated "example" is the same word used for the heading in the copybook which children used as a model in learning to write. Most of us recall the model alphabet from which we copied. We compared our own printing or writing to the standard to see how we were progressing. The sufferings of the Christian may also be compared with the Lord's suffering to see how the Christian is measuring up. We will however never reach His level of suffering. Why not? Peter goes on to show the perfect character of the One who suffered for man's sin.

Whether Peter was an eyewitness of the Lord's crucifixion is not clearly revealed in any Scripture. But it is interesting that he does not describe the Lord's sufferings on that occasion in his own words. Instead, in verses 22–25, Peter makes remarkable use of the Old Testament. There are no less than five quotations from or allusions to Isaiah 53. He reminds us in verse 22 that our Savior was sinless, for He "committed no sin." There was no deceit in him: "Nor was any deceit found in His mouth." Jesus Christ did not fail in either deed or word; therefore, He did not deserve to suffer. Obviously, He did not suffer for His own sin, but for the sin of others.

The Lord's submissiveness is seen in verse 23 in the fact that when He was unjustly attacked, He did not retaliate. When His life was threatened, He did not invoke the judgment of God on His oppressors. Instead, He said, "Father, forgive them; for they do not know what they are doing" (Luke 23:34). We are so unlike our Lord. We are quick to come to our own defense. We answer back quickly when we are unjustly criticized. We threaten our opponents when they oppress us. Christ committed no offense, and yet He suffered for us. How did He behave in this situation? He "kept entrusting Himself to Him who judges righteously," His heavenly Father (v. 23). The Son, in complete obedience to the Father, simply handed Himself over to His Father. He had already prayed for the Father's will to be accomplished (Luke 22:42). If that involved suffering and death, He knew He was in the Father's hands.

Peter makes it clear that the Father's will did include the Lord's death, because "He Himself bore our sins in His body on the cross" (v. 24). This confirms that Christ suffered because He took the penalty for sin. The sins that drove Christ to the cross were the sins of mankind: He bore our sins. The word translated "bore" was used to designate the bringing of a sacrifice to the altar. Christ died in our place and we have been set free from the bondage of sin. The phrase "that we might die to sin" (v. 24) carries the idea of getting away from something. We, as believers in the Lord's death, have been removed from the power of sin because Jesus Christ stands in our place. We should live unto righteousness as God intended man to live. We were spiritually dead, but the death of Christ has brought healing to mankind.

It is fitting that in a section addressed to Christian slaves, Peter mentions the fact that the Lord's body bore "wounds" (v. 24) from the beatings He endured. To some degree, slaves understood the physical sufferings that Christ experienced.

According to verse 25, we were like sheep that were continually going the wrong direction. The general inclination of sheep is to wander or go astray, and that is certainly the inclination of mankind. Things have changed, however, for we no longer need to wander. We have a Guide, a Guardian, and a purpose. We now follow our Shepherd (John 10:11) who tends all of His sheep. This Shepherd is also the Guardian (the overseer or bishop) of our souls.

THE CHRISTIAN AND HIS FAMILY (3:1-7)

The opening phrase in 3:1, "In the same way" indicates this section is connected with what has preceded it. The relationship that exists between the Christian and government, and the Christian and his employer, should also be found in the Christian home.

God's delegated authority in the home is given to the husband. That a wife should be in subjection to her own husband in no way implies that the wife is inferior.

The biblical principle is that, in the chain of command, God has delegated man to be over woman. This is true whether the husband is a believer or not. Just as the Christian was to be subject to a ruler like Nero or to an unreasonable employer, a Christian wife is to be subject to her husband, even if he is unsaved. Peter clearly is referring to an unsaved husband, for he says it may be possible that the husband is even "disobedient to the word" (v. 1). The Greek word for "disobey" is a strong word, and it implies that the individual has set himself against the truth. Under these circumstances, there is danger that the wife may begin to nag her husband about his church attendance or the lack of it. In her zeal to win her husband to the Lord, she may drive him away. Peter says that the wife should so submit herself to her husband that she will win him to the Lord through her manner of life, perhaps without saying a single word. Instead of "nagging" him to Christ, she should love him to Christ.

The true Christian life lived before an unbeliever should be attractive. Peter says that the husband will see "your chaste and respectful behavior" (v. 2). The life displayed before the husband will be a pure one, because it is lived in reverence for God and reverence for the husband (see Eph. 5:22–24).

The wife should live before her husband so as to emphasize inner qualities rather than external appearances. The word "adornment" (v. 3) is the Greek word *kosmos,* from which we get the word *cosmetics.* These things should not be of primary importance to the Christian woman. Peter specifically mentions the braiding of the hair, the wearing of gold jewelry, and the putting on of dresses (v. 3). The women of Peter's day went to great pains to enhance their appearance. They dressed their hair elaborately, often weaving gold and silver into it, and wore very elaborate and ornate clothing.

Peter is not saying that Christian women should never fix their hair, wear jewelry, or dress attractively, but he emphasizes the "hidden person of the heart" (v. 4). The cultivation of the inner spirit is more desirable than the ornamentation of the body. Beauty may fade, gold and silver may tarnish, and clothing will wear out, but the inner person is eternal. A gentle and quiet spirit is of great value. The gentleness of the wife describes her manner of submitting to the authority of her husband, and her quietness pictures her attitude toward her husband and life in general.

Peter mentions women in Old Testament times as examples of wifely submission (vv. 5–6), pointing specifically to Sarah. Sarah showed the proper respect for her husband, for she referred to Abraham as her "lord." Wives who follow in the train of Sarah by submitting to their husbands are called Sarah's "children" (v. 6). The final statement of verse 6, "without being frightened by any fear" is a very free translation of Proverbs 3:25–26. The idea is that a wife who submits to her husband does not need to fear anything, because she is doing that which is right. Her husband will respect her and she will also be accepted by God, who has commanded this submission.

Perhaps a word would be helpful at this point to Christian wives who are married to unsaved husbands. Peter emphasized that the Christian wife should concentrate on developing the inner person, but this does not mean she should ignore her external appearance. Verse 3 acknowledges that external adornment is one way—but not the main way—to please one's husband. However, neglecting her personal appearance will not help win her husband to Christ. Develop the "hidden person of the heart," live your life before your husband in submission, pray for the salvation of his soul, and do everything that you can to keep yourself physically appealing to your husband. Dresses, hairdos, and jewelry need not be expensive, but they should be attractive. All of these things are part of your manner of life before your husband.

In verse 7, Peter focuses his attention on the husband. He has the responsibility to "live" with his wife. The Greek word that is translated "live" is the equivalent of the Hebrew word "to know." In other words, it refers to sexual relationships. The husband is to be sensitive to the physical and intellectual aspects of the marital relationship. Perhaps this is what Paul had in view in 1 Corinthians 7:1–5. Some married people in Corinth were evidently refraining from the sexual relationship because they felt there was something evil about it. Both Paul and Peter remind the husband that the sexual relationship is a vital and holy part of a marriage, but it demands a special sensitivity on the husband's part as he considers not just his own desires and needs, but those of his wife as well.

The husband is instructed to live with his wife in an understanding way as with someone "weaker, since she is a woman" (v. 7). Notice Peter does not say that the wife is a "weak" vessel. If he had said that, then the husband would be the strong vessel and the wife would be the weak vessel. Peter says that she is "weaker." That means that both the husband and the wife are weak and need the Lord's strength in their lives. Much discussion has been devoted to the meaning of the term "weaker." Usually, but not always, the wife is weaker in terms of physical strength, but even that cannot be proven. Perhaps we will never know exactly what Peter had in mind.

Spiritually, the husband and wife are "fellow heir[s]" (v. 7) of the grace of God that leads to life. Paul says men and women are fellow heirs (Rom. 8:17; Gal. 3:28) and share God's gifts equally. In addition to what a husband and wife share physically, they share spiritual fellowship with God. For this reason, they are to enter together into all that is theirs in this life, both physically and spiritually, "so that [their] prayers will not be hindered" (v. 7). Partnership in every area of life is important. Partnership in the physical realm will produce children, and partnership in the spiritual realm will produce answered prayers. Both are essential to the married couple, and undoubtedly there is a relationship between them.

Disharmony in either the spiritual or physical sphere might affect the other sphere. We frequently think prayers are not answered because of sin in our lives, but perhaps a couple has not been faithful in their physical responsibilities to one another. Could that failure or oversight be the thing that is keeping their prayers unanswered? Only God would know the answer to that. But the human being is an integrated individual and cannot be compartmentalized into physical, emotional, spiritual, and intellectual areas, with no interrelationship among these areas.

SOME REVIEW QUESTIONS

1. What does the biblical concept of "submission" imply? Is it in any way inferiority?

2. Under what circumstances do you believe that it would be right for a believer to openly rebel against his government? Justify your answer from Scripture.

3. Can you relate an example of when your submission to your employer resulted in opportunities for your personal testimony for Christ to be made clear?

4. How does the example of the Lord's suffering speak to some situation in your life today?

5. What practical lessons have you learned from Peter's words to wives?

NOTE

1. NERO (A.D. 37–68) became the Roman emperor in A.D. 54. For the first five years of his reign, he ruled justly and with mercy, even though his personal life lacked moral restraint. Later he became cruel and vindictive, ordering members of his own family killed. He began persecuting Christians, and it is alleged that he ordered the burning of Rome and then blamed them for the destruction. According to tradition, Peter was martyred during Nero's reign.

6

CONDUCT BEFORE MEN: SOCIETY

Peter has demonstrated the practical outworking of the believer's salvation, showing the relationships that should exist between the Christian and his government, his employer, and his family. In 3:8–22, Peter gives exhortations that apply to all groups of people in a society.

Peter begins this section by writing, "to sum up," and he follows in verse 8 with a list of five characteristics or attitudes desirable in Christians. All five things pertain to social relationships.

FIVE NOBLE CHARACTER QUALITIES

First, Peter urges believers to "be harmonious," or to mind the same things. The character of a man is determined and revealed by the things to which he gives his mind. Believers in the Lord Jesus ought to be united in a common outlook and common interests. If their minds are controlled by God's Word and the Spirit, believers generally find that they are experiencing unity. Paul communicates this idea in Philippians 2:5, where he exhorts believers to have the mind of Christ. We are exhorted to unity by both Peter and Paul, but we are not exhorted to uniformity. The various parts of our physical bodies work together as a single organism, yet the individual parts have great differences of purpose and function. Believers are united in Christ, but each has his gifts and place of service for ministry.

Second, believers should be "sympathetic," which carries the idea of having compassion for one another. The Greek word Peter uses here implies the idea of suffering together. If one is selfish, it is difficult to demonstrate genuine sympathy toward a brother in Christ.

Third, believers should be "brotherly," for they are indeed related in the family of God. The churches of Jesus Christ throughout the world would be changed if the believers in them would exhibit true brotherly love. This does not imply that brethren would see eye to eye on every issue, but even in the midst of disagreements there would be genuine love. It is one thing to use uncomplimentary phrases when joking with members of one's family, but if "outsiders" use the same terms, family members are usually quick to defend the one so maligned. Is such an attitude present in the church of Jesus Christ today? Are we ready to defend fellow believers when they are criticized by unbelievers, or do we join in the criticism?

Fourth, believers should be "kindhearted," which means to be affectionately sensitive. Christians should express more affection to each other. We have lost concern for the needs of others within the church in our busy twenty-first-century living.

Finally, believers ought to be "humble in spirit," or courteous. Humility is a peculiarly biblical virtue. A picture of one's self as a weak, dependent, finite creature, should produce the proper spirit in the heart. When one truly measures himself against the perfect standard—God in His holiness—the only proper response is humility.

EXPRESSING THOSE FIVE QUALITIES

Those five characteristics should be evident in the believer's life, and Peter goes on to show how they are manifest.

The natural inclination is to strike back when struck. The believer who possesses the five qualities of verse 8 will not give back "evil for evil or insult for insult" (v. 9). This is probably an allusion to 1 Peter 2:23 and the example of Jesus Christ. To retaliate is not the biblical answer. Instead, the believer should give back blessing. The Lord taught in Matthew 5:44 to "love your enemies and pray for those who persecute you." Paul said that when he was reviled, he gave a blessing in return (1 Cor. 4:12). Peter communicates the same idea, for he says that instead of rendering evil, the believer should "[give] a blessing instead" (v. 9). The Greek word that Peter uses for "blessing" implies speaking well of those who speak evil of you. It includes the idea of bestowing blessing and even praying God's blessing on those who oppose you.

Why should the believer bless his enemies? Because God has blessed his own life; therefore, he is exhorted to extend similar blessing and forgiveness to others.

In verses 10–12 Peter quotes from Psalm 34. Many have felt that these verses contain a hymn or a part of a catechism of the early church. In describing "the one who desires life" (v.10), the apostle refers to the person who, at the end of his or her life, desires to be satisfied because of a fruitful and worthwhile ministry. As the psalmist points out, if one truly wants to experience a life that is worthwhile and meaningful, he must follow certain guidelines.

First of all, the person must "keep his tongue from evil and his lips from speaking deceit" (v. 10; cf. Ps. 34:13). Usually evil expressions are calculated to harm another person, and expressions of deceit are meant to mislead individuals. Such a tongue will not produce the kind of life the psalmist described.

Second, the individual must "turn away from evil and do good" (v. 11; cf. Ps. 34:14). Wrong deeds are usually the product of planning and deliberate choice. Instead of planning to do evil, the individual must plan to do what is good.

Third, the individual should "seek peace and pursue it" (v. 11; cf. Ps. 34:14). If the individual truly wants to control his tongue, to turn from evil and do that which is good, and to actively seek peace, he will not be giving evil for evil, or insult for insult. His thoughts will be oriented differently, and when he is attacked, he will not immediately think of ways to strike back.

Instead, he will think of ways to make peace. Peter continues to quote from Psalm 34 to summarize this section. He reminds us in verse 12 that the Lord God is aware of all that takes place in the life of the believer. He sees all that comes to pass, and He is ever open to the prayers of His children. But He also sets His face against evildoers, and His punishment will fall on them. This is the real reason that the believer is not to strike back when offended. God has not committed judgment to the Christian. The believer should follow the Lord's own example (1 Peter 2:23) and turn his case over to the Father.

RESPONDING TO PERSECUTION

Peter takes up the subject of suffering for Christ in verses 13–17. To begin, he asks the question, "Who is there to harm you if you prove zealous for what is good?" (v. 13). Peter does not deny that Christians may suffer or even be martyred, but these things do not really harm the testimony of the Christian who is seeking to do what is right. His point is that even if a believer is called to suffer, he ought to consider himself to be "blessed" (v. 14). This may seem paradoxical. The term "blessed," however, does not mean that one is delighted or filled with joy. Rather, in using this term, Peter implies that anyone who is called to suffer should consider himself highly privileged, for he is the object of divine favor. God is working in his life to teach him something.

The same message is communicated in James 1:2–4: The testing of faith produces endurance or patience in the life of the believer. Paul, in Romans 8:18, wrote that our present sufferings are nothing when "compared with the glory that is to be revealed to us" at the manifestation of our Savior. In addition, in 2 Thessalonians 1:4–5, Paul explains that our sufferings prepare us for that which is ahead. Just as parents discipline their children to teach them a lesson with regard to some specific duty, so God disciplines the believer through suffering. Whenever the child of God is experiencing God's discipline, he should consider himself "blessed," or favored. God knows the individual's capabilities, and He wants to strengthen him for some task.

In the midst of suffering, the believer should not be intimidated by what others might say (v. 14), nor should he be troubled in his heart. Instead of being disturbed, the believer ought to acknowledge Jesus as Lord (v. 15). He must recognize that the Lord controls his life and permits nothing to come into the life of the Christian that is not a part of His plan.

Since the heart is the realm in which the Christian has fellowship with God, Peter may be implying that persecution may prevent believers from worshiping together in public meetings (v. 15). Persecution from governments has from time to time forced Christians to cancel their public worship services. If public worship were forbidden today, we could enjoy fellowship with God in our homes. After all, worshiping God is a spiritual act. The place of worship is not as important as the attitude of the heart.

Even under such circumstances, the believer is admonished to "always [be] ready to make a defense to everyone who asks you to give an account for the hope that is in you" (v. 15). Peter may refer specifically to a formal defense of Christianity before the government, or he may mean an informal kind of testimony that may be called for at any time. The Greek verb implies ordinary conversation rather than an official inquiry. The phrases "always" and "to everyone" seem to make this general and comprehensive. It is not the believer who initiates the discussion, but the individual who asks the question.

CLUES TO WITNESSING

Peter gives some clues for witnessing in this epistle that seem a little strange. First, a wife is *not* to preach to her husband about the Lord, but *to win him to Christ through her manner of living* (3:1–7). Secondly, we are to be ready with an answer whenever we are asked about our faith. This is not to say that believers should never bring up the subject of salvation, for often people's questions have implications leading to a presentation of the Gospel. We should use every opportunity to reach people for Christ, and so we must be ready when they ask about our hope. Paul told Timothy to preach the Word when he was

ready—"in season"—and when he was not—"out of season"
(2 Tim. 4:2). As those who have a hope, we ought to know what
we possess and how others can share in it.

We are to witness "with gentleness and reverence" (v. 15).
An arrogant, belligerent attitude usually turns people away from
us, but gentleness or meekness and reverence may draw them in
love to our Lord. While we may not agree with others' beliefs
concerning such things as sin and salvation, we ought to approach
them respectfully and carefully. They are convinced that they
are correct, and we will never reach them by running over their
feelings. It is the conviction of the Holy Spirit, not our condemning attitude, that causes a person to accept the Lord Jesus
Christ. We ought to be reverent in witnessing because we stand
on holy ground. When the Holy Spirit brings conviction to the
heart of the individual, an eternal transaction takes place (cf.
John 16:7–11).

The life that the Christian lives before his unsaved neighbors
is vital to his witness, as Peter points out in verse 16. This is similar to what he said in 2:12. By living his life in a consistent
manner of good behavior, the Christian will put his accusers to
shame. Unbelievers may attempt to malign Christians, but if the
life of the Christian contradicts the accusations, the unbeliever
will be shamed into silence. Such patient endurance also has
value of its own. Peter reminds us that it is better to "suffer for
doing what is right than for doing what is wrong" (v. 17). The
person who suffers for doing evil is experiencing the consequences of his wrongdoing. But when a good man suffers, God
undoubtedly intends for good to come from it.

OF IMPRISONED SPIRITS, NOAH,
AND WATER BAPTISM

The final verses of chapter 3 are very difficult to understand,
and there are many interpretations of this passage. Perhaps the
following explanation will help.

In verses 18 through 22, Peter once again writes of the Lord's
sufferings. Christ's suffering is a pattern for the believer who
should count it an honor to suffer for doing what is right. Jesus

Christ had done only good, but He suffered. Christ, the Just One, suffered for the unjust. He willingly died that He might reconcile mankind to God. The believer has been presented to God on the basis of Christ's atoning blood. Jesus Christ was "put to death in the flesh" (v. 18). This suggests a violent death. The fact that Jesus Christ really died indicates that he was truly human. He was a real man and not simply a being with the appearance of a man, as some heretics taught in the early church. (For instance, proponents of Docetism taught that Jesus Christ only seemed to have a human body and that He was not a real man.)

Death, however, was not the end of the Lord, for He was raised from the dead—"made alive"—by the Spirit (v. 18). There is some debate among theologians concerning the identity of the "spirit." Some hold that this refers to the human spirit of Christ, which did not die in the crucifixion. Others hold that it refers to the Holy Spirit, the third Person of the Godhead. While either interpretation is possible, this author believes that this verse refers to the Holy Spirit. This reference to the Spirit of God leads Peter back in time.

He reminds us that it was through the Holy Spirit that Christ once preached to "spirits now in prison" (v. 19). Exactly who are these "spirits" who are in prison? Some believe that this is a reference to an act Jesus Christ performed between the time of His death and resurrection. They take the position that Jesus Christ went to the spirit world, or the residence of the spirits of the dead, and announced that He had accomplished victory over Satan. However, this view has not been satisfactory to many. Why would Christ announce victory to people whose eternal destiny had already been sealed? This interpretation causes further difficulty, for it implies the doctrine of a second chance.

It is the belief of this author that the phrase "spirits now in prison" is explained in verse 20. These "spirits" were the people living in the days of Noah, when he was building the ark. These were the people mentioned in Genesis 6:5–6: "Then the Lord saw that the wickedness of man was great on the earth, and that every intent of the thoughts of his heart was only evil continually. The Lord was sorry that He had made man on the earth, and He was grieved in His heart" These were the rebels who rejected the testimony of the Lord through the witness of Noah. It is stated in the Genesis account of the Flood that Noah spent over one hundred years constructing the ark, and every nail he drove into the ark should have warned the men living in that time of the coming judgment. Since they refused the testimony of the Lord through Noah, the Flood came to destroy them.

Therefore, they were confined to the place of departed spirits to await the final resurrection of the wicked at the Great White Throne judgment of God (Rev. 20:11–15). Peter could say that the Lord preached to "spirits now in prison," for when he penned these words, the spirits of these people were confined.

The Flood reminded Peter that not everyone living in those days was judged by water. Eight persons were "brought safely through the water" (v. 20) because of their faith in God that caused them to enter the ark. Therefore, the ark became, in Peter's thinking, a picture of salvation. In the church age, the corresponding figure is baptism. Just as the ark pictured salvation for Noah, baptism pictures the salvation experience for the believer today.

One interpretation of baptism here is that Peter is referring to the baptizing work of the Holy Spirit, which places the believer into the body of Christ, the church (1 Cor. 12:12–13). While this is a possible interpretation, this author believes that the ordinance of water baptism is more appropriate in light of the context, which certainly seems to contain a lot of water. This is not to say Peter believed a man is saved by water baptism, for the phrases that follow do not support such an interpretation. Peter says that baptism is "not the removal of dirt from the flesh" (v. 21). The filth of our sinful natures can never be removed by water. The ordinance of water baptism is dependent on "an appeal to God for a good conscience" (v. 21). The response in the heart of the believer is what is most important. The ordinance of water baptism reflects externally that which has taken place within the believer's heart.

Perhaps Peter had in view here the pledge that Christians in the early church took at the time of their baptism. Baptism pictures the death, burial, and resurrection of Jesus Christ, as Peter points out in the concluding phrase of verse 21.

The Resurrection was God's approval of the work of the Son on the cross. Now He is exalted, standing at the right hand of God. Paul says that the *man* Christ Jesus is our intercessor in heaven (1 Tim. 2:5). His place is one of supreme privilege and immediate access to the Father, for He is in the continual presence of His Father. At this present time, all heavenly beings (angels, authorities, powers) are subject to Him. Someday all who live on earth will acknowledge His authority, for "at the name of Jesus every knee will bow, of those who are in heaven and on earth and under the earth, and that every tongue will confess that Jesus Christ is Lord, to the glory of God the Father" (Phil. 2:10–11).

There is some evidence that these phrases at the end of 1 Peter 3 were part of a baptismal formula that was repeated by a person as he was baptized. Careful examination of verses 21 and 22 shows that it would be difficult to honestly repeat what Peter has said unless one were a true believer. Notice that within this section Peter has mentioned the death, resurrection, and ascension of the Lord. That Peter fully understood the doctrine of Christ cannot be denied.

SOME REVIEW QUESTIONS

1. What five characteristics does Peter emphasize as being desirable in every Christian's life? How would you grade your own life on these qualities?

2. What application does Peter make from Psalm 34? Does his use of this psalm strike a responsive note in your heart?

3. What is the paradoxical truth connected with the suffering of the believer?

4. What does it mean to acknowledge Jesus as Lord in your heart?

5. What are the possible explanations for the phrase "the spirits now in prison"?

7

CONDUCT BEFORE MEN:
CHRIST'S EXAMPLE

The fourth chapter of 1 Peter continues the discussion of the Christian's relationship to his fellow men. First Peter 3 concluded with the sufferings of Christ, and this subject is carried into chapter 4. The example of Jesus Christ in His suffering should inspire the Christian to strength and purity in his own life.

LIKE CHRIST IN SUFFERING

Peter reemphasizes the main lesson from 3:16–22, which is that Jesus Christ suffered for us in the flesh. We should keep in mind that the Lord Jesus not only suffered for us, He actually died for us. What should be the Christian's response to the Lord's action? He ought to equip himself with the same mind that Jesus Christ had toward suffering. Peter mentioned the "purpose" (attitude) of Jesus Christ toward suffering in 2:21–25. The last phrase of 4:1 helps us see what the attitude of the Christian should be in suffering. If we suffer in our flesh as Jesus Christ suffered, we have "ceased from sin," or perhaps a better translation, we have ceased to do evil.

The Christian who stands true to Christ during persecution does not do evil. He will not strike out in retaliation, for he will withstand persecution as Christ did. Christ could have called for legions of angels to come to His defense (Matt. 26:53), but He submitted to His captors. Christ never gave evil for evil, and the Christian who has the attitude of Christ toward suffering will not strike out against his persecutors.

LIKE CHRIST IN PURPOSE

Peter continues this thought into verse 2. He says that the Christian should not live his life ("spend his life" in the Greek text) following "the lusts of men, but [according to] the will of God." These two philosophies are directly contrasted in the text. The person who does not know God is driven by his desires to satisfy his own appetites. But the Christian who has the proper perspective on life enjoys a singleness and clarity of purpose that the unsaved individual can never experience. The Christian does not live to gratify fleshly desires, but to accomplish the will of his Father in heaven.

In this we are like Jesus, who always sought to do the will of His Father. That was the focus during His sample prayer early in His ministry (see Matt. 6:10), and it remained the focus during His final prayer in Gethsemane (see Matt. 26:39–44).

Before accepting Christ, the Christian might have been completely absorbed in following "the lusts of men" (v. 2). In verse 3, Peter lists six worldly pleasures: (1) "sensuality" (unbridled, lustful excesses); (2) "lusts" of various kinds (see 2:11 and 4:2); (3) "drunkenness" (literally, overflowing of wines); (4) "carousing;" (5) "drinking parties;" and (6) "abominable idolatries" (idolatrous acts improper even by the world's standards). Perhaps both Gentile and Jewish leaders were guilty of these worldly kinds of things.

Since those who have accepted Christ can no longer participate in their former sinful practices, their unsaved friends do not understand them. According to verse 4, the unsaved are surprised that their old friends no longer run around with them. Christians who have been saved out of a wicked background know exactly what Peter is talking about. Since coming to know the Lord, they no longer enjoy the old sinful "fun" with their friends. Unsaved individuals therefore sometimes talk about their Christian friends and invent unjust and malicious stories about them. Perhaps Peter is giving us an illustration of Christians who are reviled for their well doing. The Christian has done nothing to warrant such an attack, but the unsaved judge the Christian's life and find him to be out of line with their worldly standard. Peter reminds us that one day they shall be called into account before almighty God. They make their judgments based on incomplete knowledge, but they shall be called into account by the One who knows all things.

Possessing perfect knowledge, God is qualified to judge all men, whether they be living individuals or those who have died. We know from other Scripture that God the Father has appointed Jesus Christ to be the Judge (John 5:22, 27; Acts 17:31; Rom. 2:16). Since Jesus is the Father's appointed agent, His judgment is ultimately a judgment from God the Father. All men will meet God one day in the person of Jesus Christ. Those who accept Him will meet God as Savior, but those who reject Him will meet God as Judge. The Gospel which has been proclaimed to mankind will be the basis for judgment.

Peter says the Good News has been preached "even to those who are dead" (v. 6). But what does he mean by "dead"? Some believe that this refers to men who are spiritually dead. However, the context seems to imply physical death. The same word for "dead" was used in the previous verse to refer to those who are dead physically. Some believe that men who do not hear the Gospel in this life will have a chance to hear it after their death. But this interpretation presents a difficulty, for it implies the doctrine of a second chance. The best view seems to be that Peter uses the term "dead" to refer to individuals who heard the presentation of the Gospel when they were living, but now at the time of writing are dead. (This would be consistent with Peter's usage of "the spirits *now* in prison" in 3:19.) The point is that these individuals have heard the Gospel, but they have rejected it. However not all men reject the truth of the Gospel. Some who hear the Good News in their flesh begin to "live in the spirit according to the will of God" (v. 6). Those who have turned their backs on the practices mentioned in 4:3 would be good examples. Not all men reject God's grace; some turn to the Lord for salvation. That fact will be a condemning factor in God's judgment on the others.

The thought of the Lord's coming judgment reminded Peter of the fact that prophetic events could be set in motion at any time. He says that "the end of all things is near" (v. 7). John the Baptist used the same word (Matt. 3:2), and Jesus used it of the kingdom which was about to be instituted on the earth if men would believe (Matt. 4:17). James uses this expression in relation to the Lord's return (James 5:8). Peter here also says that the return of the Lord is imminent. This should prompt all believers to action, for the time remaining could be indeed short.

In view of the possibility of the Lord's return, Peter admonishes the believers to be "of sound judgment" (v. 7), or to be of a sound mind. This verb is used in Mark 5:15 of the demoniac at Gadara, who after being delivered from his demonic possession by Jesus was said to be "in his right mind." Soundness of mind is a vital aspect of the believer's life, but Peter also admonishes the believer to have a "sober spirit for the purpose of prayer" (v. 7). Such a spirit is indispensable to full prayerfulness. A Christian should keep himself awake and alert with complete control of his faculties so that he can give himself to prayer. Of all people, the Christian should not allow his mind to become confused or dazed by drink or drowsiness.

The individual in complete control of his mind is able to have the proper perspective. The Christian who is not sound in his judgment or sober in his spirit is apt to be praying more for his wants than for his needs. God has promised that He will provide the latter (Phil. 4:19) but not the former. Sobriety in praying will undoubtedly lead to praying only for those things that are in the will of God. Therefore, the Christian may have confidence in prayer (1 John 5:14–15).

LIKE CHRIST IN LOVE AND SERVICE

Sobriety and informed prayer are important, but Peter says that "above all" (v. 8), Christians should "keep fervent in [their] love for one another." He assumes that love exists among Christians, and his admonition is that love should be strenuously maintained. The word "fervent" has the root idea of stretched or strained. It is used to describe, for example, an athlete straining his muscles in an effort to accomplish his goal, or of a horse running at a full gallop. The word suggests intensity of effort, or the exerting of one's powers to the fullest extent. More important than any other thing, believers should practice love fervently. This mark identifies a real Christian (1 John 4:7–11).

Love "covers a multitude of sins" (v. 8). What does Peter mean by this? He seems to imply that the Christian who is demonstrating true love will be willing to forgive a fellow brother in Christ over and over again. After all, this is how God treats us, and we ought to treat other believers in the same way. Jesus has called on us to forgive again and again, telling Peter to forgive 490 times (Matt. 18:21–22)! He set the example, forgiving Peter after the apostle three times denied knowing Jesus (Matt. 26:69– 75).

Peter does not mean that sins in our own lives are forgiven because we love our brothers, but that our love for fellow Christians enables us to overlook their sins. The sins covered are those of the one loved, not the one loving. True love accepts the person just as he is, faults and all. This does not imply that the local church should never deal with gross sins, but that the Christian should never hold past sins against a brother who has turned his back on those sins.

Love should also be manifested in hospitality toward one another (v. 9). To extend hospitality toward a fellow believer is a concrete demonstration of love to him. In Peter's day, many who professed faith in Christ were cut off by their families and needed a place to live. In addition, many traveling missionaries and evangelists needed lodging. The inns were dreary, filthy places that were reputed to house perpetrators of every kind of immoral act. Traveling Christians needed to stay with fellow Christians or they could not continue their work. The exhortation to hospitality still holds in our twenty-first-century world.

But hospitality was often thrust on the same people over and over. Not every member's home in the church was large enough to accommodate visitors. Peter therefore urges that hospitality be shown "without complaint" (v. 9), or murmuring. Continual grumbling by the host has a way of spoiling the hospitality that is extended. Some might feel resentment over having to entertain a constant stream of visitors, but Peter reminds them that hospitality is an opportunity to show love for the brethren. This is a form of service to Jesus Christ Himself. Peter implies that such a ministry may be undertaken in complete confidence that the Lord will provide all that is needed, and such service will bring great reward (see also 3 John 5–6; Heb. 13:2; and 2 Cor. 9:6–8).

First Peter 4:10 admonishes all believers to exercise their spiritual gifts. We ought to minister because we all have received "a special gift." The idea found in Peter's words, "employ [your gift] in serving one another," is rendering all kinds of service to others. The Greek verb was used in Acts 6 for the serving of tables. The exercise of spiritual gifts is part of the Christian's stewardship, because God has equipped each one to perform certain tasks. Since each member of the Christian community has been divinely empowered for service, we all have a corresponding responsibility to use our gifts properly. If we fail to do our part, the body of Christ suffers and someone else must pick up our slack. These gifts for service demonstrate "the manifold grace of God" (v. 10) in the lives of believers. The Greek word for "manifold," which also occurs in 1 Peter 1:6 and in James 1:2 [translated "various" in both references], means "many-colored." Each gift demonstrates a facet of God's grace as the possessor uses it to minister to others.

What are these gifts? While Peter does not list specific gifts, Paul enumerates them in three separate passages (Rom. 12:6–8; 1 Cor. 12:27–31; Eph. 4:7–16). It is not possible to discuss each of the gifts in detail in this book, but the reader is urged to consult these passages. Every Christian can possess at least three spiritual gifts: (1) the gift of giving, (2) the gift of showing mercy, and (3) the gift of helps or ministry.

In verse 11, Peter mentions two types of Christian ministry. One is through the spoken word, involving preaching or teaching. This ministry ought to employ "the utterances of God." This term is used elsewhere in the Scripture to refer to the words that come from God's mouth. The preacher or teacher ought to proclaim the words spoken by God Himself.

A second type of ministry is simply called "serving," and sometimes it is referred to as "ministry." We must never forget that ministry takes many forms. Helping people in various ways is ministry! Setting up chairs for a church function is ministry! Stuffing church bulletins on a Friday morning is ministry! All of us can be involved in serving, performing it "by the strength which God supplies" (v. 11). The verb "supplies" here has the idea of equipping people for a task. God, who has infinite resources, enables believers to use these resources to the fullest in the exercise of their gifts. Whether it be public preaching or teaching, or private serving, the motivation for using a spiritual gift is to give glory to God. God should be the One who is glorified through the use of one's gifts, not the individual. Since the ability to minister is a gift, and the strength for the ministry comes from God, why should any individual boast?

This thought caused Peter to respond with a doxology to God through Jesus Christ, "to whom belongs the glory and dominion forever and ever" (v. 11). Peter's "Amen!" is a form of endorsement and we ought to translate it, "So be it!"

SHARING IN SUFFERING WITH CHRIST

The final section of this chapter (vv. 12–19) deals with the Christian's witness in the midst of suffering. Peter says that we should not be amazed or surprised by our "fiery ordeal" (v. 12). The trial of the believer is like the refining process of metal. The intent is to prove its value, not destroy it. Perhaps Peter's Gentile readers were shocked by the persecutions they were called on to endure for Christ. Gentile believers probably had never been persecuted, for as unbelievers they were worshiping according to an approved religion of the Roman Empire. But now as "Christians" they were following a "religion" that the Empire did not recognize. Their resulting persecutions might cause them to wonder about the promised blessings of the Gospel.

Peter says that the Christian ought to rejoice and keep on rejoicing, because he is being permitted to share the sufferings of Christ. The persecution of the Christian should indicate to him that he is on the right road.

When we suffer for God, we are like Christ, who suffered that He might honor the Father. If we are sharing in the sufferings of Christ, we shall also share in His glory. The Savior entered this glory by way of suffering, and one day His glory will be manifested to the world. The prospect of sharing in Christ's glory causes us to rejoice now, even though we may be in the midst of suffering. Perhaps we are being "reviled for the name of Christ" (v. 14). The paradox of the Christian experience is that in the midst of being reproached for Christ's sake, the Christian experiences happiness. This happiness is a deep, abiding joy, stimulated by the realization that God is working in the Christian's life.

Peter says that "the Spirit of glory and of God rests on you" (v. 14). Probably Peter is referring to the Shekinah glory of God, which rested on the tabernacle and in the temple in Old Testament times. This was a special manifestation of God's presence with the people, and such a manifestation is present today among God's children in the person of the Holy Spirit.

However, a Christian may suffer for his own sins. Peter mentions two specific crimes, murder and stealing (v. 15). He also uses a general term, "evildoer" (v. 15), used previously in 2:12 and 14. He admonishes the Christian not to be "a troublesome meddler" (v. 15). This is a very interesting term, which Peter apparently made up himself. The word "meddler" is derived from the word for "bishop." Perhaps some preachers were meddling in the work of other preachers. Preachers, however, are not the only ones guilty of this offense, and Peter urges all believers to avoid it.

It is interesting that Peter, who urges us "not to be ashamed" to bear the name of Christ (v. 16), was himself ashamed of his association with the Lord. Although Peter denied his Lord, he was restored. We may be confident of finding the same forgiveness for sin.

Peter reminds us, in verse 17, that God is going to judge all things, and His judgment will begin with His own. If His judgment brings the believers earthly suffering (as it does in some cases) what must be the punishment of the unsaved? Their final end is really too terrible to contemplate. The salvation that God has provided for mankind cost God a great deal, for it involved the death of His Son. The destiny of the unbeliever who rejects what cost God so much can never really be visualized or expressed.

Christians should remember that suffering in this life may be according to the will of God. Instead of wondering if we can endure, we should commit ourselves to God who is able to give victory in any situation. Let us put our trust in the One who created all things.

CONCLUSION

The believer's relationship to other men and women has been the major subject of 1 Peter 2:13–4:19. Because God loved and saved us, we are responsible for loving others, even as Jesus did. May this practical portion of the book be instructive to each of us.

SOME REVIEW QUESTIONS

1. What are some of the main things that characterize an individual's life before and after accepting Jesus Christ as personal Savior?

2. Why does a believer find that former sinful habits often no longer have the same appeal in his life?

3. In view of the possibility of the Lord's imminent return, how should a believer live his life?

4. What role can hospitality play in the life of a believer? Do you have the gift of hospitality?

5. What contribution does Peter make to the discussion of spiritual gifts in the body of Christ?

8
CONDUCT IN THE CHURCH

Peter has given a thorough analysis of the believer's relationship to God and to his fellowmen. Another area to which Peter gives special attention is the church. He devotes the final chapter in his first epistle to this subject.

CONDUCT OF THE PASTOR (5:1–4)

Peter begins this section with an address to those who are responsible to care for the local congregation, "the elders" (v. 1). The word "elders" in the original text is *presbuteroi,* which seems to emphasize the status of these individuals as the senior leaders of the church. This author believes that the terms "elder" (*presbuteroi*), "overseer" (sometimes translated "bishop"), and "pastor" (sometimes translated "shepherd") refer to the same individual in the church. All three terms are apparently used interchangeably in Acts 20:17, 28. There Paul is speaking to the "elders" (v. 17) whom he had summoned to Miletus. He reminds them that the Holy Spirit had made them "overseers, to shepherd the church of God which He purchased with His own blood" (v. 28). The term "overseer" or "bishop" is a title, and the term "pastor" refers to the job of shepherding.

Referring to himself as being an elder, Peter admonishes his readers as one who is familiar with the job. As an apostle he could have ordered them to follow his instruction, but he does not take that approach. His appeal instead is based on the fact that he is one of them and thus understands their problems. As one who shares the same responsibilities, he urges them to be devoted to their duty.

Peter is more than a "fellow elder," however, for he was one who had been privileged to be a "witness of the sufferings of Christ, and a partaker also of the glory that is to be revealed" (v. 1). The term "witness" does not mean to be a spectator, but it refers to one who presents a testimony. It is impossible to present a testimony, however, unless one has been a true witness. The fact that Peter had viewed some of the sufferings of the Lord Jesus placed a great responsibility on him to share what he had seen. Not only had he seen the Lord's sufferings, but he had also been a partaker, or a sharer, in His glory. One day this glory of the Lord will be manifested fully to the entire world, but Peter had been privileged to see a glimpse of it during His life on earth. It is generally agreed that Peter is referring to the incident that took place on the Mount of Transfiguration, when the glory of the Lord was revealed to the inner circle of disciples: Peter, James, and John (cf. Matt. 17:1–8, Mark 9:1–8, and Luke 9:28–36).

Peter's admonition to his fellow elders seems to echo the Lord's admonition to Peter before the Ascension. Peter urges them to "shepherd the flock of God among you, exercising oversight" (v. 2). In John 21:16, the Lord said the same to Peter. The verb for "shepherd" in the original text denotes the work of a shepherd in caring for his flock. The job of the shepherd includes many joys as he provides for the flock, leading it to food and water. But the job also includes unpleasant tasks, which are part of the total responsibility. Peter's admonition is to oversee the flock and not neglect the sheep. Because the position of shepherd includes problems as well as joys, the one who labors simply under a human call will soon quit the flock. The faithful shepherd is one who has responded with a willing heart to God's call to the job of shepherding.

The motivation for the shepherd should not be "for sordid gain" (v. 2)—that is, merely for financial return. But Peter does not imply that the shepherd should not be paid. The fact that some were desiring sordid gain implies that the ministers of Peter's day were paid for their labor.

The shepherd is not to establish himself as a dictator over the sheep, nor should he be "lording it over those allotted to [his] charge" (v. 3). Rather, he is to be eagerly leading the sheep by example. He should be "proving [himself] to be examples to the flock" (v. 3). The idea is not that the flock should merely be looking to a man, but that, as the shepherd looks to the Lord and walks closely with Him, the sheep also will follow Him closely.

In verse 4, Peter exhorts the shepherd to be faithful because one day he must give an account for all his actions with the flock. Since the elders are not dealing with their own sheep, they are really "undershepherds," those who care for the flock of Someone else. There is coming a time when every undershepherd will give an account to the "Chief Shepherd," who undoubtedly is the Lord Jesus Christ Himself (John 10:11). When the Chief Shepherd returns, the undershepherds will be rewarded for their faithfulness with "the unfading crown of glory." What a responsibility rests on the elder! What a glorious prospect awaits those who faithfully feed the flock which God has entrusted to their care!

CONDUCT OF THE PEOPLE (5:5–11)

In this section, Peter examines the responsibilities that rest on all the members of the congregation. Just as the elders must give an account of all their actions, all believers will be called into account before God. Therefore, Peter urges believers to practice willing subjection and submission toward each other by giving honor to one another. This admonition is undoubtedly directed toward all members of the congregation, but it is aimed particularly at the younger members (referred to as "younger men" in verse 5). They are urged to submit themselves to the older members. The implication of this is that all should be willing to be subject to one another. This is difficult and cannot be accomplished in human strength. As Paul states in Ephesians 5:18–21, such subjection comes only when people are filled with (controlled by) the Holy Spirit.

Peter further admonishes his readers by saying "and all of you, clothe yourselves with humility toward one another" (v. 5). The Greek word translated "clothe" denotes putting on a garment such as an apron. Peter draws the analogy here of putting on humility as though it were an apron. In light of the context of submitting to one another, it is entirely possible that Peter is referring to the incident that happened in the Upper Room (John 13:1–17) when Jesus rose from the table, girded Himself with a towel, and humbled Himself before the disciples by washing their feet. Each believer should have this attitude toward other believers and willingly submit himself to them.

To drive his point home, Peter quotes from Proverbs 3:34 to show that humility is a virtue that God desires all men to have. All men would do well to remember these words: "God is opposed to the proud, but gives grace to the humble." We live in an age when men are proud and arrogant. God notes the actions of men, and He deals with them according to their works. He sets Himself against the proud, but to the lowly He grants favor. Peter therefore exhorts believers to "humble [them]selves under the mighty hand of God" (v. 6). Deliberate self-subjection ought to be the practice of the child of God toward his Father. One who really understands who God is, and who sees himself in the light of that understanding, has no difficulty in humbling himself. An awareness of God's sovereign control over our lives leads to humility.

To those who do humble themselves under God, Peter says that God "may exalt you at the proper time" (v. 6). What a promise! Note that this exaltation comes in God's time, not man's. In fact, for most Christians exaltation probably will not come in this life. Paul says "that there were not many wise according to the flesh, not many mighty, not many noble" who are called (1 Cor. 1:26). But God's exaltation of the humble will come when He chooses to bring it to pass.

The thought that exaltation does not always come in this life reminds us that this life is filled with cares. The Christian is not freed from the problems of the world. Many problems arise, and the believer is not able to solve all of them. In verse 7, Peter reminds his readers that there is a remedy for the "anxiety" that arises from problems. Anxieties can disrupt the believer's mind and decrease his devotion to God, but he is exhorted to throw them on God. Many religions teach that the worshipers must appease their god in order to find his favor. It is a distinctive promise of Christianity that *God cares for the believer.* The Christian may bring all of his anxieties to God and leave them with Him, assured of the fact that He does care.

This truth is a source of comfort and peace, but many Christians never enter into the enjoyment of it. They know this teaching, but the adage, "Why pray when you can worry!" is the theme of their lives. Such Christians are like the "double-minded man" of James 1:8. They bring their problems to God but they cannot completely release them. Do such people really believe God? Are they really casting their cares on Him?

Carelessness in the life of the Christian should never be tolerated. The Christian needs to be self-controlled and alert. Peter urges sobriety and vigilance on the believer's part because of his "adversary" (v. 8). The Greek word for "adversary" carries the idea of an opponent in a lawsuit. When this term is applied to Satan by Peter, the picture of the heavenly courtroom is brought into focus. According to Revelation 12:10, there is rejoicing in heaven at about the midpoint of the seven-year tribulation period because the accuser of the brethren, Satan, is finally cast out of heaven. It is said there that he is the one who has been accusing the brethren "before our God day and night."

The fact that Peter refers to Satan as "the devil" shows what kind of accuser he is. The word "devil" means slanderer. Satan, our present opponent in the heavenly courtroom, is undoubtedly not presenting the facts truthfully. However, the believer has an "attorney" who defends him in that same courtroom. According to 1 John 2:1, Jesus Christ is the "Advocate" who pleads the believer's case before the Father.

The implication in Peter's statement is that Christians are giving Satan the ammunition he needs to accuse us before the Father. We must be alert in order to avoid aiding our adversary.

Satan is also pictured as a "roaring lion" (v. 8) stalking about seeking to destroy his prey. The lion would like nothing better than to destroy the Christian. He is out to ruin as many believers as possible. The roar of a lion can strike terror in the heart of a man. Should the Christian flee from the enemy? Peter's admonition is to "resist him, firm in *your* faith (v. 9). This is a command! Cowardice never wins against Satan, but courage does. The phrase "firm in your faith" implies being solid as a foundation. Ephesians 6:10–18 mentions the weapons that the believer may use in his battle with the forces of Satan. The key is that the victory is won through the power of God, not the power of the individual. Peter depicts this conflict with Satan as a great battle that is taking place among all of the brethren. This battle is intended for the purpose of perfecting the Christian.

Peter's words to the congregation of the church remind us that we worship "the God of all grace" (v. 10). His grace covers every need and is available to every member of the Christian family. The God who has called us to eternal glory in Christ Jesus also cares for our present needs. It is part of His glorious plan that believers may suffer "for a little while" (v. 10), but "the sufferings of this present time are not worthy to be compared with the glory that is to be revealed to us" (Rom. 8:18). The prospect that awaits the believer makes suffering in this life bearable.

It is Peter's prayer (v. 10) that his readers might be "perfect," or complete (mature); that they might be "confirm[ed]," or steadfast (solid as granite); that they might be "strengthen[ed]," which probably means equipped for active service; and that they might be "establish[ed]," or perfectly at peace with God and men.

The concluding verse of this section may be called a doxology, since verse 11 does not have a verb in the original language. It is best understood as the language of prayer with the "Amen" adding an emphatic endorsement: "So let it be!" The noun "dominion" is used only of God in the New Testament. It describes the quality of keeping under control or retaining mastery. This power belongs to God for all time and eternity.

CONCLUSION (5:12–14)

The final three verses of 1 Peter may have been written by Peter in his own handwriting. The implication in verse 12, "through Silvanus, our faithful brother (for so I regard him), I have written to you briefly," is that Peter dictated this letter to Silvanus, who copied it down. This was a very common practice in biblical times. Even today business executives do not compose their own letters but assign them to administrative assistants. But Peter may have penned these final verses as his mark of authenticity for the readers who would recognize his handwriting. Silvanus was undoubtedly known to the readers of this letter, for he was considered a faithful brother. Peter concurs with this opinion because he had come to know Silvanus' character and work through personal contact.

This short letter had a twofold objective: to give exhortation and to testify concerning "the true grace of God" (v. 12). Peter undoubtedly had the gift of exhortation and used it here through the written word. He desired to confirm these believers in their faith and to encourage them to stand firm even in the midst of suffering. Also, he wanted to testify to God's grace, both in his own life and in the Gospel he was proclaiming.

Personal greetings are exchanged in verse 13. The text literally says, "She who is in Babylon." And as noted in chapter 1 of this book, this is probably a greeting from Peter's wife to her friends. As a believer in Christ, Peter's wife would have been elected to salvation along with the readers. Since both translations are possible, and since the question has no definite solution, no authoritative statement should be made. In light of the statement, "and so *does* my son, Mark," it seems more probable to this author that Peter was referring to his wife. Mark is undoubtedly John Mark who was not the natural son of Peter. But if the greetings are being sent from "she" and "Mark," and since we know for certain that Mark was a living person, does it not make sense that the "she" should also be a living person?

A final note, from the depths of Peter's heart, is that the believers in the congregation ought to demonstrate their affection toward each other. The "kiss of love" (v. 14) was a sign of unity and love exchanged by the believers when they met for worship. In our western culture the handshake has replaced this custom.

Peter concludes with a prayer for peace for all believers in Jesus Christ. Peace is the traditional Hebrew benediction. True peace is possible only for those who are in Christ. The blessing and fellowship of the Gospel rests completely on a personal relationship with the Messiah. Apart from Him, these blessings can never be fully realized, but in Christ all of the blessings of God may be enjoyed.

SOME REVIEW QUESTIONS

1. Are you involved in a shepherding ministry with any group of people? What reward might you look forward to as a result of this kind of ministry?

2. What are some of the qualities Peter emphasizes for all of us as members of local churches?

3. Is there biblical evidence to support the idea that God always vindicates His children in this life?

4. Who does Peter say is "the adversary" of the believer? How can this adversary be defeated?

5. Although suffering might be the believer's current condition, how does Peter picture the future prospect for that suffering individual?

SECOND PETER

OUTLINE OF THE EPISTLE OF 2 PETER

I. INTRODUCTION (1:1–2)
  A. The author (1:1A)
  B. The addressees (1:1B)
  C. The greeting (1:2)

II. CHARACTERISTICS OF THE CHRISTIAN LIFE (1:3–21)
  A. Protection (1:3–4)
  B. Progression (1:5–11)
  C. Proclamation (1:12–21)

III. CAUTION IN THE CHRISTIAN LIFE (2:1–22)
  A. Features of the False Teachers (2:1–3)
  B. Figures OF Old Testament judgment applied to the false teachers (2:4–11)
  C. Future of the false teachers (2:12–22)

IV. CONFIDENCE IN THE CHRISTIAN LIFE (3:1–16)
  A. Peter's aim (3:1–2)
  B. Peter's admonition (3:3–7)
  C. Peter's assurance (3:8–16)

V. CONCLUSION (3:17–18)

9

CHARACTERISTICS OF THE CHRISTIAN LIFE: PROTECTION AND PROGRESS

For years critics have attacked the authority of 2 Peter. A close examination of this epistle will show why some have been opposed to it, for Peter takes a strong stand against those who would depart from the faith which he had been teaching. With that in mind, let's begin by determining the actual authorship of this important epistle.

INTRODUCTION (1:1–2)

THE AUTHOR (1:1A)

As we begin 2 Peter, we notice that the introduction differs markedly from that of 1 Peter. In the second letter, Peter uses his full name, "Simon Peter," whereas in 1 Peter, he simply called himself "Peter." This difference causes the critics to theorize that these letters were written by different men.

However, this difference can also be used as a strong argument for the authenticity of the epistle. If 2 Peter were the product of a forger, he certainly would not have departed from the recognized Petrine introduction. The apostle Peter, however, felt no compulsion to use the same introduction for each letter. How

do you sign your letters and notes? Is that decision not completely in your hand? But would a forger take the liberty to change
from your known signature?

Peter not only used his Hebrew name Simon (or Symeon in
some manuscripts) in the opening of his second letter, he also
referred to himself as "a bond-servant and apostle of Jesus Christ."
A person's self-description is interesting, for it reveals many things
about him or her. Peter regarded himself as a servant, a bond
slave, of Christ. The Greek word for servant is *doulos,* indicat-
ing one who is in bondage to another. Peter did not feel ashamed
of the fact that Christ was his master, and that he was nothing
more than a slave. But Peter did have authority, for he was also
an apostle, a "sent one." The joining of these two ideas combines
the personal humility of Peter with the authoritativeness of his
apostolic position.

THE ADDRESSEES (1:1*b*)

First Peter was written to those of the Dispersion, those who
had emigrated to lands surrounding Palestine. Apparently Peter
wrote his second letter to the same group of people (see 2 Peter
3:1), although the group had grown larger. Second Peter was
addressed to all those who have obtained "a faith of the same
kind as ours." This "like faith" is one word in the Greek text,
meaning "equal in honor and privilege." This word was used
for foreigners who had been granted citizenship and were equals
with natives. These readers who were once spiritual foreigners
(both Jews and Gentiles) have been privileged to become citizens
of heaven, just as Peter had. This was accomplished through
"the righteousness of our God and Savior, Jesus Christ," and
not through human merit. Peter was firmly convinced that Jesus
Christ was God and that He was the Savior of all mankind.

THE GREETING (1:2)

Peter's greeting to his readers is brief but extremely significant. He uses the normal Greek and Hebrew greetings, "Grace
and peace be multiplied to you," but he adds that grace and

peace can come only "in the knowledge of God and of Jesus our Lord." The insertion of the word "knowledge" is significant. The people to whom Peter was writing were being deceived by individuals who claimed to have a true knowledge of God and of Christ, but who exhibited immoral behavior. Quite possibly "knowledge" was one of their catchwords, and Peter uses that word to attract attention. He was not afraid to make that word a key part of his vocabulary.

The Christian life is never static, but it is a growing thing. Growth is dependent on the knowledge of God and Christ. As the Christian acquires greater knowledge, grace and peace will be multiplied in his life.

CHARACTERISTICS OF THE CHRISTIAN LIFE
(1:3–21)

PROTECTION (1:3–4)

In verse 3, an appeal for holy living by the believer is centered in God's calling the believer to His own glory. God has provided all that is necessary for the believer to lead a godly life. Peter traces success in the Christian life to the knowledge of the Lord Jesus Christ who called us, and especially to a realization of His "glory and excellence." These attributes have drawn the individual to Christ. The word "excellence" refers to the Old Testament sense of virtue in action, or concrete deeds of excellence.

The person of Jesus Christ attracts men and women, and His power enables them to respond. Because of Christ's glory and virtue, believers have been given "precious and magnificent promises" (v. 4). Peter seems to imply that believers have been given the promise of sharing Christ's moral excellence in this life, and His glory in the hereafter. Through Him, believers "may become partakers of the divine nature" (v. 4). The believer is able to have perfect fellowship with the three persons of the Trinity. This fellowship is initiated through personal relationship with Jesus Christ and offers hope for the future as well as escape from the corruption of the world. Corruption basically comes through "lust" (v. 4). Each person must make a choice. Either he becomes freed from sin, or he becomes further enslaved to sin.

It should be noted that in verses 3–4, Peter uses a number of daring words rarely found in the New Testament, but full of meaning in the pagan world. He emphasizes *knowledge, godliness,* and *excellence.* He speaks of *divine power* through which it is possible to lead a holy life and escape the corruption of this world. Since these terms were pagan in origin, some have questioned whether this book ought to be included in the canon of sacred Scripture. But Peter undoubtedly was trying to reach his audience. He did not want them to stop after reading the first two verses. He flavored his letter with words that would catch their attention and cause them to continue reading to see what he had to say.

PROGRESSION (1:5–11)

The believer has the promise of God regarding his life and the future, but Peter stresses the believer has obligations in this life. That is why he begins verse 5 by saying "for this very reason." God has provided the believer with the necessary power to live the Christian life, but the believer cannot sit back and relax. The grace of God demands that the believer apply "all diligence," or effort. The word translated "applying" here implies "adding on your part." Peter is saying "because of all that God has done for you in your life, add, on your part, real effort." The Christian life is like the use of power steering on a car. The engine provides the power for the steering, but the driver must actually turn the wheel. So the Lord provides the power to run our lives, but we must "turn the wheel." To a great extent, the Christian determines the course of his or her life.

The Christian life begins, of course, with faith (v. 5). The initial acceptance of God's love, which was demonstrated by the death of Christ, is the foundation stone. To this foundation, Peter says, the believer is to "supply" certain things. The English word "supply" does not adequately express the meaning of the Greek. The word used in the original spoke of an individual who underwrote the expenses of the choruses in Greek plays. Therefore the word came to picture "generous and costly cooperation." Thus Peter implies that the Christian ought to willingly and actively cooperate with God in order to produce the Christian life.

What qualities are to be added? Seven are listed in verses 5–7. They are:

1. *Moral excellence* (v. 5). As we explained above in connection with verse 3, "excellence" implies the idea of virtue in action, or concrete deeds of excellence. Since believers are privileged to share the moral excellencies of the Lord, they ought to manifest these qualities in daily living.

2. *Knowledge* (v. 5). Peter probably is referring to practical wisdom. Although wisdom was one of the catchwords of the false teachers, note that Peter was not afraid to use it. Since God is the source of all truth, the Christian need never fear the truth. The cure for false knowledge is not less knowledge, or a retreat from knowledge, but more knowledge. It is significant that knowledge was included in the list of characteristics, and that it appears after faith. Faith is never achieved through the mental process only, but is founded on knowledge. Faith apprehends that which knowledge cannot comprehend.

3. *Self-control* (v. 6). This word is not common in the New Testament, but was used in Greek moral philosophy. It meant to control one's passions rather than to be controlled by them. The Christian's key to achieving temperance is submission to the Holy Spirit (Eph. 5:18).

4. *Perseverance* (v. 6). Self-control will result in "perseverance." This word means to voluntarily and continually endure difficulties and hardships for the sake of honor. James used this same word in his letter (James 1:3) when he said that "the testing of your faith produces endurance." This Greek word used by both men is used elsewhere in the language to describe swords. If a sword possessed the quality of "perseverance"

or "endurance," it was an instrument that had the ability to withstand blows. If the believer has cast his anxieties on God (1 Peter 5:7), he will not panic over difficulties and distress. Rather he will be able to take the blows and to withstand.

5. *Godliness* (v. 6). Godliness results when an individual carefully observes the requirements of God on his life. This is the same Greek word Peter used in verse 3 where he stated that God's divine power has given the believer everything that he needs for godliness. Paul told Timothy to discipline himself "for the purpose of godliness" (1 Tim. 4:7, same Greek word). If the believer is growing in his godliness, he truly will find increased devotion to God in his daily experience. This will result in perfect peace between the believer and God.

6. *Brotherly kindness* (v. 7). Godliness does not exist in a vacuum, however. The believer who is right with God will demonstrate his "brotherly kindness" through acts of righteousness. First John 4:20 declares: "If someone says, 'I love God,' and hates his brother, he is a liar; for the one who does not love his brother whom he has seen, cannot love God whom he has not seen." Love for the brethren is one of the distinctive marks of the Christian. It can be manifested in many ways and should be demonstrated in new ways continually.

7. *Love (charity)* (v. 7). Peter teaches that the crown of the Christian's progress is love, *agape* in the Greek text, which is defined as the deliberate desire for the highest good in the one loved. Such love is essential to the Christian community.

This is the list of virtues that should be growing in the life of the believer: moral excellence, practical wisdom, self-control, perseverance, godliness, brotherly kindness, and unselfish love. When the believer looks at such a list and at his or her own life, the first reaction might be to give up. However, we should remember that there is a cooperative effort between the believer and God as they work together to produce these qualities. The important question for each believer to ask personally is not, *Do I possess all of these qualities in my life* but, *Are all of these qualities present and growing in my life?*

Peter continues his exhortation to believers by demonstrating both the result of following his suggestions and of ignoring them (vv. 8–9). Christians who possess a true knowledge of Jesus Christ and who allow these qualities to be manifest in their lives will find that those qualities will continue to grow.

There can never be room for spiritual self-satisfaction, for no believer ever "arrives" spiritually. But on the other hand, the Christian who ceases to grow in his or her Christian life begins to regress. The abounding Christian will discover that he or she continues to produce spiritual fruit (cf. John 15:1–8). But Peter sees this entire process of growth centered in "the true knowledge of our Lord Jesus Christ" (v. 8). Our Christian life (1) begins in the knowledge of God and of Jesus (v. 2), (2) continues in the knowledge of Him who calls us (v. 3), and (3) will end in the full knowledge of the One who makes all these virtues possible (v. 8).

There might be those who fail to follow Peter's exhortation concerning the matter of Christian growth. Peter declares that Christians who fail to make this progress in their lives are "blind" (v. 9), lacking spiritual insight. They fail to see the struggle going on between themselves and the forces of evil and thus do not equip themselves for the battle. Paul declares, in 2 Corinthians 4:4, that Satan blinds the mind of unbelievers to keep them from believing on Christ. Peter's implication is that some believers are blind in failing to recognize the need for growth in their lives.

Peter adds that such believers are "short-sighted" (v. 9). This is a strange idea, for if someone is blind, he cannot see at all. Peter may be implying that such a person is blind in that he has lost sight of his heavenly calling. Since the verb form for "short-sighted" can also mean "to blink," or "to shut the eyes," Peter may be implying that the Christian who fails to grow is blind because he has deliberately shut his eyes to the light. The second rendering is supported by the next phrase in verse 9, which declares that such a person has "forgotten his purification from his former sins." This verb implies that the individual had deliberately put out of his mind the fact that his former sins have been removed. The "former sins" undoubtedly refer to sins committed before conversion. Such a person makes no effort (v. 5) to grow in grace. The consequences of this for one's spiritual life could be most severe.

By his entire argument, Peter urges his readers to exert themselves and to make certain of their calling and election (or "choosing"). In verse 10, he repeats the call for zeal that he gave in verse 5. The tense of the verb in this passage stresses the urgency of his appeal. He again states clearly the need for cooperation of the human will with God's sovereign call. Election originates with God, but man's behavior confirms that election. Christian calling and Christian living must not be separated. Believers who confirm their calling by their conduct will be aware of two results. The first result relates to this life: Such believers "will never stumble" (v. 10). Christians who progressively develop these virtues in their lives will grow steadily. This growth will be obvious proof that they have been elected by God.

The second result relates to the future. Peter says these believers will reach the goal of his lifelong journey, for his "entrance into the eternal kingdom of our Lord and Savior Jesus Christ will be abundantly supplied to [him]" (v. 11). This picture was borrowed from the Greek culture. Heroes from the Olympic games were welcomed back to their home cities in a spectacular way. They were not brought through the regular city gate, but through a special one constructed for the occasion. Therefore, the believer who follows the Lord's program for growth will be abundantly blessed in the future. He will share in the everlasting kingdom of Jesus Christ, which will one day be manifest on the earth.

SOME REVIEW QUESTIONS

1. Does the different introduction of 2 Peter argue against the authority of the book or for the discrediting of the work?

2. Peter's appeal for holy living at the outset of this book is centered in what?

3. How does faith relate to all phases of the Christian life?

4. What role does the believer have when it comes to the development of the Christian life?

5. Peter anticipates the results that will occur in those who heed his suggestions and those who ignore them. List both the positive and negative results.

10
CHARACTERISTICS OF THE CHRISTIAN LIFE: PROCLAMATION

The Christian's life should be a proclamation of the truth that the Christian knows. In 2 Peter 1:12–21, Peter states that during his life he has sought to confirm the community of believers in the great truths he had come to know.

PROCLAIMING TRUTH

The "therefore" that begins verse 12 links this section with everything that Peter has said so far, especially the sure calling and election of the believer, which form the basis for his or her life of witness. Peter's goal in life was "always [to] be ready" in presenting the truth, and to use every opportunity to instruct others in the faith. In Peter, we see a great example of restoration. He who is now so concerned about diligence had once denied his Lord. During the night when Jesus was arrested, Peter three times denied that he knew Him (see Luke 22:54–62). Perhaps this is one reason for Peter's determination to never again deny his Lord. His goal was "to remind [believers] of these things" (v. 12), that is, of the great themes of the Christian life.

That Peter was reminding them of certain truths implies that these letters contained no new revelations from God (although they were inspired!). These reminders were truths that Peter had taught his readers previously in personal contacts. In this way, Peter fulfilled his position as an elder (see 1 Peter 5:1–4).

One important function of a Christian minister is to continually remind his congregation of basic Christian teachings. Sadly, many Christians are ignorant of these teachings and therefore they do not live by them. But a greater problem is that many Christians do not live according to the truths they do know. Peter was not writing to immature believers, but to people who had been "established in the truth" (v. 12). Even mature Christians may lapse into serious sin and doctrinal error. The truth is to be safeguarded by the faithful minister who continually instructs his people in the Word. Peter was doing this in an attempt to keep his readers established in the truth.

The fact that Peter believed it was his solemn duty to witness for the Lord is emphasized in verse 13. Perhaps he was remembering the Lord's words spoken to him in Luke 22:32: "I have prayed for you, that your faith may not fail; and you, when once you have turned again, strengthen your brothers." He compared his earthly life in verses 13 and 14 to living in a tent, a "tabernacle," according to the King James Version. This idea was used in connection with the Lord Himself in John 1:14, "And the Word became flesh, and dwelt [tabernacled] among us." A tent is not a permanent structure. It can be taken down and moved quickly. This figure, translated "earthly" in the NASB, expresses the idea that life is transitory; therefore, one must buy up every opportunity.

PROCLAIMING UNTIL DEATH

Peter's intent was to "stir up" (v. 13) his Christian brothers and sisters. The Greek word he used for "stir up" was often used of awakening someone from sleep. Peter wanted to keep the Christians of his day awake and alert. The reason for the urgency of Peter's exhortation was his realization that his death was near. Peter undoubtedly had in mind the words of the Lord as recorded in John 21:18, "'Truly, truly, I say to you, when you were younger, you used to gird yourself and walk wherever you wished; but when you grow old, you will stretch out your hands and someone else will gird you, and bring you where you do not wish to go.'" Verse 19 goes on to explain that by these words the Lord was signifying "by what kind of death he [Peter] would glorify God."

The text does not tell us why Peter was convinced that his death was near. Perhaps he was imprisoned in Rome at this time and knew his death was imminent. Perhaps the Lord Himself revealed it to him. Peter uses a graphic word for death; he calls it his "departure" (v. 15) from the earth. The Greek word he chose is sometimes translated as "exodus" or "exit." He saw death as moving from this life to another life. It was taking down his tent and moving it to another location. This word was also used of the Lord's death in Luke 9:31. It is stated that on the Mount of Transfiguration, Moses and Elijah spoke with the Lord "of His departure which He was about to accomplish at Jerusalem." The word Luke used for "departure" is the same word Peter uses.

Even in the face of his death, Peter felt responsible to proclaim what he knew about the Lord. Therefore, he took steps to ensure that even after his death believers would "be able to call these things to mind" (v. 15). What these steps were is not certain. Many believe that Peter was referring to the young man, John Mark. In the first letter, Peter mentioned that Mark was with him in "Babylon" (1 Peter 5:13). Mark may have traveled with Peter during the last years of his life, and during this period, Peter filled his mind with his recollections of his time with Jesus.

PROCLAIMING AS AN EYEWITNESS

It has been suggested by some that Peter was preparing Mark to write a biography of the Lord Jesus' life, which we now possess in the gospel of Mark. Many have called Mark's account "The Gospel of Mark According to Peter." It is interesting that Mark includes facts about Peter that are not contained in other gospels. The theory that the gospel of Mark reflects the teachings of Peter is feasible. Peter's teachings would be reliable and accurate since he had followed the Lord as one of the twelve apostles. In verse 16, Peter declares: "For we did not follow cleverly devised tales when we made known to you the power and coming of our Lord Jesus Christ, but we were eyewitnesses of His majesty." Paul declared, in 1 Timothy 4:7, that false teachers were guilty of giving attention to "worldly fables." Peter claims that he never followed a cleverly devised deception, which contained some of the truth. His goal was to proclaim faithfully the power of the Lord to equip Christians for holy living and the future coming of the Lord.

The word that Peter uses for "eyewitness" (v. 16) was ordinarily used of one who had been initiated into the secret practices of the mystery religions of that day. Through this word, Peter discredits false teachers who claimed that they had been initiated into a higher knowledge. These teachers could never know what Peter knew because they had not experienced what he had seen.

What is Peter talking about when he claims to have been an eyewitness of the majesty of the Lord? According to the verses that follow (17–18), this statement refers to Jesus' transfiguration (see Matt. 17:1–9; Mark 9:2–9; Luke 9:28–36). The Synoptic Gospels reveal that of the twelve apostles, only Peter, James, and John were permitted to witness that event. Obviously Peter was well qualified to talk about the particulars on that occasion. The three apostles heard the voice of God from heaven, which testified to the person of the Son. The presence of God was also manifested through "the Majestic Glory" (v. 17). Perhaps this means that the voice of God was manifested through the excellent glory of the heavens. Or, "the Majestic Glory" may be the bright cloud that overshadowed Jesus at that time. The latter is probably the better explanation. The cloud was the equivalent of the Shekinah glory of God that was over the tabernacle and the temple.

The voice of God actually spoke from this cloud and said, "This is My beloved Son with whom I am well-pleased" (v. 17, cf. Matt. 17:5). The voice gave credence to all that Jesus Christ had taught in His earthly ministry, and confirmed that He was the very Son of God. It is interesting to note that the gospel accounts of the voice differ from the account in 2 Peter. It is the author's opinion that this difference strongly supports the argument that Peter wrote 2 Peter.

Since he actually witnessed the Transfiguration, Peter was not limited to previously recorded accounts of that event. In 2 Peter, the complete statement of the voice is not given. The additional words as recorded in all three gospel accounts, "Listen to Him!" are omitted. It is not likely that a forger, copying this story from the gospels, which were recognized as authentic, would have departed from the standard texts. Peter, however, as an eyewitness, would not be forced to copy from other manuscripts.

In verse 18, Peter refers to the place of transfiguration as a "holy mountain." He considered this place especially holy because the glory of Jesus Christ was revealed there. God visited it in the person of the Son, and also in the person of the Father who testified to the Son. The transfiguration of the Lord made a life-changing impact on the apostle Peter.

PROCLAIMING THE SURE WORD OF GOD

His comment in verse 19, "We have the prophetic word made more sure," has been interpreted in various ways by Bible teachers. It seems to this author that Peter is comparing the written Word of God, the Scriptures, with the experiential testimony that he has been presenting. He had just talked, in verse 15, about sharing, through John Mark, what he knew of Christ and his explanation of what took place on the Mount of Transfiguration. He seems to anticipate a reply: "But that's been *your* experience, Peter, but *my* experience does not agree with yours." His answer is that if his personal word is rejected, there still is a testimony that is more sure, the Word of God.

Peter is, in effect, saying, "If you won't believe what I have said, then believe what is written in the Word of God." Peter obviously believed that his understanding of the life of the Lord Jesus agreed with the Old Testament. He compares Holy Scripture to "a lamp shining in a dark place" (v. 19). A person is foolish to stumble around in a dark room when there is light available. Someone who does not believe Peter's personal testimony may seek the light of the Scripture and attempt to understand it for himself. Peter was not afraid of submitting that which he taught to close scrutiny in light of the Scriptures. He believed his testimony would stand the test.

We must continue to rely on this Word until "the day dawns and the morning star arises in your hearts" (v. 19). According to Revelation 22:16, Jesus Christ is this morning star. Peter's argument is that we as believers walk in a dark world. Our only light is the light of His Word. But there is coming a day when the full light of the revelation of God will shine in our hearts, a day when we shall see Him as He is. Then we, too, shall be like Him.

In verse 20, Peter declares that "no prophecy of Scripture is a matter of one's own interpretation." This verse has caused some difficulty because of the word "interpretation" in the English translation. Some believe that this verse teaches that the individual should not try to interpret or understand the Scriptures for himself. They say, "Private interpretations lead to errors, because an individual cannot understand the total teaching of the Word. Only the church's leaders can properly interpret the Scriptures." But in this author's understanding of Peter's argument, the subject under consideration is not the interpretation of the Word, but rather the source of the Scriptures. The idea might be more clearly conveyed if the verse was translated, "no prophecy of Scripture is a matter of one's own origination."

The Scriptures were not produced by the minds of the men who wrote the text. In 1 Peter 1:10–12, Peter states that the prophets many times did not understand what they actually wrote. It was possible for them to communicate the truth even though they did not understand it. Here in verse 21 Peter says that "no prophecy was ever made by an act of human will."

But God did not communicate His truth through just any man. It is clear that the writers of the Scripture were special men whom the Lord equipped to communicate His truth. They wrote only as they were "moved by the Holy Spirit" (v. 21). The word "moved" which Peter uses to describe the cooperation of the divine and the human in the production of the Scriptures was also used of sailing ships that were blown along by the wind. The writers of the Scriptures were carried along in the writing of the text by the "wind" of God, the Holy Spirit. The picture here is one of God utilizing men in the production of the Word. The writers of the text were not passive in the reception of the truth, but neither were they the originators of the truth. The personalities of the authors were not violated, but the direction which they took was controlled by the Holy Spirit.

Paul teaches that the Scriptures are literally "God-breathed" ("inspired by God"; 2 Tim. 3:16). As God breathed out His creative breath, the Holy Spirit guided the writers of the Scripture along so that they put down on the page without error exactly what God wanted communicated.

CONCLUSION

Peter's first chapter in his second letter presents a strong challenge to the believer today. While the believer is secure in his life because of all the promises of God, he is responsible to continue to grow in his Christian life and to share with others what he has received. The key is, of course, the Word of God, and this is compared to a light, which shines in a dark place and guides the believer until the day he meets his Savior face-to-face.

SOME REVIEW QUESTIONS

1. What is a very important function of a Christian minister toward his congregation?

2. How did Peter know that his death was imminent?

3. What steps was Peter taking to make sure that his remembrances of Jesus Christ would be passed on? Did he succeed?

4. What use did Peter make of the event in Jesus' life known as the Transfiguration?

5. What role did Peter see the Holy Spirit playing in the inspiration of the Scriptures? To what did he liken the Spirit?

11

CAUTION IN THE
CHRISTIAN LIFE

The peril presented by false teachers demands that believers be always alert. In chapter 2 of Second Peter, Peter examines the problem of false teachers.

FEATURES OF THE FALSE TEACHERS (2:1–3)

Peter begins by reminding his readers that in the past, many false teachers arose in the nation of Israel, and they may be expected in the church as well. Falsely claiming to be prophets, these individuals also make false prophecies. They secretly bring in their "destructive heresies, even denying the Master who bought them" (v. 1). They do not walk in the front door of the church and teach false doctrines openly, but they sneak in through the back door to secretly spread their insidious doctrines.

Their greatest error is their denial of the Lord who paid the price for their sins. The Greek word *agorazo*, translated "bought," carries the idea of paying a price for redemption. Peter believed that the death of the Lord paid the redemptive price for even these individuals who deny the Savior. Because they have made no personal application of the redemption, these individuals bring on themselves "swift destruction" (v. 1). The Greek word translated "swift" is the same word Peter uses in 1:14 when he refers to his death as being imminent. Those who persist in the path of open opposition to the Lord might travel the same road as Peter, that is, their death might occur at any moment.

False teachers are dangerous because many in the church "will follow their sensuality" (v. 2). The word translated "sensuality" contrasts with "the way of the truth" also mentioned in this verse. A second problem connected with false teachers is that "the way of the truth will be maligned" (v. 2). Those in the church who are immoral bring great discredit to the Christian cause. If those who are supposed to be Christians live unrighteous lives, what good is their religion?

Peter discusses the motives of false teachers in verse 3: "And in their greed they will exploit you with false words." In their desire to make money, they say whatever they think their hearers will accept. The Greek word translated "exploit" is derived from a commercial background. It carries the idea of "making money from," or deriving commercial gain. These false teachers use Christianity only for financial profit. Such a motive is not appropriate to a minister of the Word of God (1 Peter 5:2). Peter says that God is aware of this situation, and His judgment will fall on those who pervert the truth. While they believe they will escape punishment, Peter shows that God's judgment will fall.

FIGURES OF OLD TESTAMENT JUDGMENT APPLIED TO THE FALSE TEACHERS (2:4–9)

Peter believed the same judgment that had been poured out in past ages on wickedness would fall on these false teachers. To illustrate his point, he cites three examples of God's judgment from the Old Testament. Two lines of truth are obvious: (1) the certainty and terror of God's retributive justice, and (2) the loving care of God and His remembrance of His children.

Peter's first example of the certainty of God's justice is the "angels when they sinned" (v. 4). God did not overlook their sin, but He banished them to a place called "Tartarus" in the Greek text, or "pits of darkness" in the English text, where they will remain until the day of their final judgment.

There is disagreement among Bible scholars as to which group of angels Peter has in mind. One interpretation is that Peter is writing about those angels who followed Satan in his original rebellion against God (see Isa. 14:12–15; Ezek. 28:15; cf. Rev. 12:3–4). However, if Satan and the sinning angels were confined until the day of their judgment, Satan and his demons would not be free today to roam the world enticing men to sin. A second interpretation is that Peter is referring to the terrible sin mentioned in Genesis 6 in which some of the wicked angels who followed Satan in the fall cohabited with the women of the earth (see also Jude 6). This sin was so terrible in the eyes of God that He confined the participating demons to Tartarus where they await their final judgment. The context in 2 Peter, which includes the Flood and the cities of Sodom and Gomorrah, seems to support the second interpretation, even though that view produces a number of difficult questions. Whichever interpretation one follows, the point regarding the false teachers is the same. Just as God judged the angelic realm, so He will judge these false teachers.

Peter's second example of God's judgment within human experience is Noah and the Flood. The sinfulness of the entire world was so great that God's judgment had to fall. But His loving care for His children is evident in that He spared "righteous" Noah and seven other persons. Peter refers to Noah as "a preacher of righteousness" (v. 5). First Peter 3:19–20 implies that Noah preached to the men of his day. The Old Testament does not call Noah a preacher of righteousness, but it does declare that he was "a righteous man, blameless in his time," who walked with God (Gen. 6:9). His way of life was different from all the wicked men around him.

Peter's point is obvious. The way of righteousness is the way of life; the way of wickedness is the way of death. The righteous man, Noah, lived through the Flood; the ungodly people perished in the water.

The cities of Sodom and Gomorrah are the third example of

God's judgment. Peter says that God transformed these cities "by reducing them to ashes, having made them an example to those who would live ungodly lives thereafter" (v. 6). The Greek word translated "ashes" was later used in secular literature to describe the destruction of Pompeii and Herculaneum in A.D. 79. Those cities were covered by lava from the eruption of Mount Vesuvius. Condemned by God, the cities of Sodom and Gomorrah are a classic illustration of the ultimate ruination of unrighteousness. False teaching ultimately results in destruction.

Note that the concern of God for His people was manifested even in the destruction of those two wicked cities, for the Lord delivered "righteous Lot" from the city (v. 7). Peter's description of Lot as a "righteous" man is actually quite surprising. The account of the destruction of Sodom and Gomorrah in Genesis 19 does not seem to picture Lot as a "righteous" man. But according to Peter, Lot was "oppressed by the sensual conduct of unprincipled men" (v. 7). The word "oppressed" means exhausted, and some scholars even go so far as to translate this word "tortured." Lot was greatly distressed by the wicked behavior he saw in the city of Sodom, but he did not move out. It is possible for a Christian to live close to sin, but he may barely escape with his life.

Peter has given three illustrations of God's judgment, one from the angelic realm and two from the human realm. His entire argument concerning the false teachers is summarized in verse 9. The two main ideas from his illustrations are (1) that God can deliver the godly from temptation, as exemplified by Noah and his family and Lot, and (2) the Lord reserves punishment for wickedness, as illustrated by the demons who sinned, those who perished in the Flood, and the cities of Sodom and Gomorrah.

FUTURE OF FALSE TEACHERS (2:10–22)

Peter's illustrations of God's judgment point out that God will ultimately bring His wrath on false teachers. In 2:10–22, Peter assures his readers that the false teachers have not escaped God's control, and he goes on to describe them and their future.

He declares that false teachers are "those who indulge the flesh in its corrupt desires" (v. 10). This phrase in the original text implies the idea of sodomy and a desire for that which is sordid. Not only are these individuals perverted in their concept of sexual expression, they also "despise authority" (v. 10). "Authority" is basically the Greek word for "lordship." Some believe that this refers to 2:1, which points out that the false teachers deny the lordship of Jesus Christ. Within this context, it is probably better to understand this as a disregard for delegated authority in the local church. These individuals are "daring, self-willed, [and] they do not tremble when they revile angelic majesties" (v. 10). If Peter has in view the authority of the local church leaders here, the expression "angelic majesties" probably is a reference to the leaders of the local church. The term "angel" basically means "a messenger," and the leadership of local churches can be considered as God's messengers today. Each church letter in Revelation 2 and 3 is addressed to "the angel [or the messenger] of the church."

Peter's point is that these false teachers are not afraid to speak out against God's delegated authority, which could be authority in the church or simply angelic authority. This is something in which angels, who are more powerful than men, would never indulge (v. 11). They would not accuse other angelic leaders before the Lord. Whatever Peter has in mind here, the main teaching is that the false teachers are continually criticizing others.

These false teachers do not follow the example of angels, since Peter declares that they live "like unreasoning animals" (v. 12). They follow the dictates of their passions and openly speak evil about things of which they are ignorant. It may be that Peter is referring to the idea of Christian restraint, which they ridicule. Since they behave as animals following their passions, the only option is to destroy them. Thus their own corruption brings about their destruction.

According to verse 13, they will receive a reward for their labors, but it will be a reward of unrighteousness, since they have sowed unrighteousness. One illustration of their unrighteousness is that they think it is "a pleasure to revel in the daytime." To participate in daytime orgy was not considered acceptable by even pagan Roman society, but these individuals participated openly, in daylight hours, in the most despicable forms of sexual behavior.

Peter applies several descriptive phrases to these false teachers, beginning in the middle of verse 13. He declares that "they are stains and blemishes." This is in direct contrast with what the apostle Paul says about the church in Ephesians 5:27, for the Lord is going to present the church "in all her glory, having no spot or wrinkle or any such thing; but that she would be holy and blameless."

According to verse 14, the false teachers have "eyes full of adultery," or more accurately, eyes full of adulterous women. In other words, they lust after every woman they see. They view each woman as a potential adulteress. Peter declares that they can never cease from such sin, for they have so continually dwelt on it that it has become their way of life. They cannot look on a woman without considering the likelihood of her sexual performance. Their hearts have been "trained in greed," an expression that was used of an unbridled desire for more and more things. This desire often included things the individual had no right to claim, including money and sex. Peter's conclusion concerning them is that they are "accursed children." He is implying that God's curse is on them, for these men have failed to trust in Christ and are leading others astray.

Peter explains how these individuals came to be under the curse of God. He begins with the fact that some have deliberately forsaken the right way and have gone astray (v. 15). They are comparable to Balaam, an Old Testament Gentile prophet (Numbers 22–25). "The way of Balaam" is a phrase used in other portions of Scripture and refers to the fact that Balaam "loved the wages of unrighteousness." Based on the account of Balaam's life, we know that he was covetous and concerned with financial remuneration. Such prophets focus primarily on the money they can accumulate through their unrighteousness. Peter pointed this out in 2:3. God rebuked Balaam through his donkey (v. 16). Peter contrasts the muteness of the animal with the madness of the prophet. The message of the donkey made more sense than the prophecies of Balaam.

As if these derogatory phrases were not enough, Peter continues his attack on false teachers. He declares that they are "springs without water and mists driven by a storm" (v. 17). Both of these metaphors would be very meaningful to people who live in an extremely dry country. Finding a well of water in the middle of a desert brings great joy. But imagine what happens when people find that the well is dry. When rainfall may be a matter of life and death, people watch with despair if clouds blow past without dropping rain. Like the mists, false teachers appear to offer a great deal, but do not produce. For such individuals the "black darkness has been reserved" (v. 17). This expression refers to the place where the angels that sinned (see 2:4) are found. Their prospects are not good.

The false teachers talk of Christianity, but they do not produce its fruits. Verse 18 says that they speak out "arrogant words of vanity." A clever way to confuse people is to use words that no one understands. True scholars do not resort to such tactics. Rather, true scholarship is the ability to explain in simple terms that which is difficult. Not only do false teachers use big words, but also they "entice by fleshly desires, by sensuality." They are out to catch people, and the bait on the hook is sensuality. The Greek word for "fleshly desires" is best expressed by the idea of "shameless immorality." These false teachers were encouraging Christians to be freer in the expression of their Christianity. Perhaps they were even suggesting that one's religion could be better expressed in a sexual way. Today they would undoubtedly be talking about free love, with all of its manifestations.

The greatest misfortune connected with false teachers is that they corrupt others. Those most strongly influenced by them were "those who barely escape from the ones who live in error." The kinds of people Peter is talking about here are those who have just shaken themselves free from pagan associations. These relatively new Christians were not yet grounded in discerning truth from error; therefore, they could be easily deceived.

The false teachers were having quite an effect on the newborn Christians because they offered liberty. Ironically they were offering something which they themselves did not possess. Being "slaves of [their own] corruption" (v. 19), they were not free. Peter reasons that it will be very hard on the false teachers, because they have been associated with Christianity yet have not been changed by it. It is the conclusion of this author that the subject of verses 20 and 21 is the false teachers, not the new believers. These false teachers have escaped "the defilements of the world" because of their associations with the church. But to go back into the world system brings about an inexcusable situation.

Peter teaches throughout these verses that it would be better to have never known the way of truth than to know it and then depart from it. The idea of knowing the truth but turning from it brought to his mind (in verse 22) two proverbs which aptly describe the behavior of the false teachers. The first of these probably reflects Proverbs 26:11. The dog that has rid himself of corruption within returns to that corruption to enjoy sniffing it. Another illustration is the pig which has been scrubbed but returns to the manure heap. It is interesting that both of these comparisons are used in Matthew 7:6 by Jesus Christ to describe those who are out of touch with the Lord. Peter undoubtedly believed that these false teachers were out of touch with God.

CONCLUSION

Peter has written in detail about the false teachers who were beginning to threaten the flock of God. He was concerned with them, as they were infiltrating the church and beginning to lead astray new converts. His bold, direct approach should be an admonition to us today as we encounter those who would seek to destroy the church. False teaching must be faced head-on, and steps must be taken to stop it while there is still opportunity.

SOME REVIEW QUESTIONS

1. What are some of the qualities of false teachers that Peter warns his readers about?

2. How do the three illustrations of God's judgment in the Old Testament relate to the false teachers? What lines of truth are clearly evident?

3. In what sense does Peter say the false teachers do not follow the example of the angels?

4. What are some of the very descriptive phrases Peter uses to picture the false teachers?

5. What is probably the worst misfortune connected with the false teachers?

12

CONFIDENCE IN THE CHRISTIAN LIFE

In 2 Peter 3, Peter turns from discussing the false teachers to encouraging the faithful. In doing so, he reveals his goal, issues a warning, and offers a welcome reassurance to a hurting church.

PETER'S AIM (3:1–2)

Peter mentions this as "the second letter" (the book of 1 Peter being the first letter) written to the same group of readers. He refers to his readers four times in 2 Peter 3 as "beloved." In both of his letters, his aim was the same: He was "stirring up [their] sincere mind[s] by way of reminder" (v. 1). He had taught them these things previously when he was with them. He was not primarily instructing his readers about new subjects, but he wanted them to remember those truths that would change their lives.

"The words spoken beforehand by the holy prophets and the commandment of the Lord and Savior spoken by your apostles" (v. 2) would produce this change. Peter's authority came from the prophets and the apostles. Clearly, he believed in the unity of the Scriptures. It was the Old Testament prophets who had foretold the coming of the Lord, and the apostles who had proclaimed that which had taken place when the Lord did come. The apostles proclaimed the words of the Lord to that generation and explained what He meant. Peter was drawing a contrast between the false teachers, discussed in 2 Peter, and true prophets and apostles. His readers were probably torn over the question of whom they should follow.

PETER'S ADMONITION (3:3–7)

Peter believed that it was crucial to warn the believers concerning scoffers who would come. The phrase in verse 3, "Know this first of all," also used in 1:20, means that what he is about to say is very important. "In the last days mockers will come" who will walk after their own lusts. Since Peter believed that he lived in the last days, believers today may surely consider that the last days are at hand. One characteristic of the last days is that those who lead self-indulgent lives will doubt the coming of the Lord. It seems that they deny the Lord's coming because they find it to be a ridiculous idea.

The scoffers argue that "*ever* since the fathers fell asleep, all continues just as it was from the beginning of creation" (v. 4). Some scholars believe that "the fathers" means the first church fathers, such as Stephen and James, the son of Zebedee. However, since this phrase is used in connection with the beginning of the creation, more likely it refers to the earliest Old Testament fathers. The scoffers repudiated the promise of His coming because, they said, things do not change. The universe is a stable, unchanging system, and God does not intervene in the course of history. The day in which we live seems to be characterized by a denial of the Lord's return. Twenty-first century man rarely thinks about the Lord's return to earth, and his manner of life reflects his disbelief.

While the scoffers argue that God does not intervene in history, Peter makes use of history to refute that argument. He says their argument has overlooked one very important event—the Flood—which shows that God does indeed intervene in human history. But the scoffers have overlooked it willingly. The earth was created by the word of God, for He spoke and it was accomplished. Peter obviously believed in a fiat creation, or the idea that all things have been created out of nothing (cf. Heb. 11:3). This was all due to the divine word of God. Peter did not hold an evolutionary concept of creation, with the act taking place over millions or billions of years.

By God's word, the earth was separated from heaven and it stood "out of water and by water" (v. 5). Some believe that this implies that a water canopy surrounded the earth in the early days of its existence, protecting it from the harmful effects of the sun. This water canopy perhaps created a "hothouse" effect which made possible the tropical plants and the large reptile like creatures which we know as dinosaurs. Some even cite this canopy as the reason for the longevity of man as described in the early chapters of Genesis. But the Flood brought about a great change in the earth's climate and topography. The world as it existed in the days before the Flood perished, because the earth was "flooded with water" (v. 6). This was obviously a direct intervention by God into the course of history.

The earth, as we know it, will one day undergo an even greater change. The judgment of the earth by fire described in verse 7 refers to the day when God will come to judge the earth and destroy all evil. (This is called the Day of the Lord in the Old Testament.) Peter envisions the great and final judgment of the earth. After the judgment of the wicked, the new heavens and earth will be created. God changed the course of history in the past by sending the Flood; and following the millennial kingdom on the earth, He will again change history by refining the earth with fire.

We may reasonably conclude that the Lord Jesus will intervene in history by His second advent to institute His kingdom on earth. In spite of the fact that the Lord has not yet returned, the hope of His return is a present reality for the believer. The Flood and the future renovation of the earth by fire remind the believer that God accomplishes what He purposes, and He has declared that Jesus Christ will come again some day (Acts 1:11).

PETER'S ASSURANCE (3:8–16)

Peter admonishes believers not to forget that "with the Lord one day is like a thousand years, and a thousand years like one day" (v. 8; see Ps. 90:4). What people regard as a long time is as one day to the eternal God. God and man have different perspectives. While many think that the long silence of the heavens indicates that God is not going to act, God views the time as though it were a moment. Even though God delays, He does not forget.

Peter reminds us that "the Lord is not slow about His promise" (v. 9). The word "slow" carries the idea of impotence, or the inability to accomplish that which one has purposed. God does not lack the strength to accomplish His goals, for He is omnipotent. Therefore God does not delay His coming because He is weak. Rather, it is His patience toward mankind that keeps Him from returning. First Peter 3:20 declares that the Lord was patient in the days before the Flood and that this patience kept the waters of the Flood from covering the earth sooner. He gave people ample opportunity to repent and to turn from their wickedness. God does not desire that anyone perish, whether it be in the days before the Flood or today.

God's wish is for all to turn to Him (see 1 Tim. 2:4). To those who repent, He is ready and willing to show His mercy. He has not returned today because He is still giving men time to turn from their wickedness to Him. But a day is coming when the patience of God will end, and the Day of the Lord will come on the earth. Since no one knows the beginning of this time, the Day of the Lord will come "like a thief" (v. 10). The coming of a thief is almost always unexpected. The Day of the Lord may refer either to the Rapture[1] of the church to heaven or to the coming of the Lord with His saints to establish His kingdom on earth, which is known as the Second Advent. It is possible to interpret this verse either way and for interpretation to make sense. The Rapture is referred to as this kind of an event (1 Thess. 4:13–18) and the Second Advent is also (Matt. 24:27–31). The only difference is whether one believes the tribulation is part of the Day of the Lord, or whether the Day of the

Lord means only those events connected with His return to earth to reign.

While the Day of the Lord will begin secretly, it will conclude with the great change that Peter mentioned in 2 Peter 3:7. The "heavens will pass away with a roar and the elements will be destroyed with intense heat, and the earth and its works will be burned up" (v. 10). This earth that we consider to be so substantial will not endure eternally, for the earth and the elements of which it consists will undergo a great change.

In verse 11, Peter turns to make a very practical application from the fact that the earth will be destroyed. He, together with all the writers of the Scripture, see a direct link between doctrine and life. All of these events will take place just as Peter has stated, and this truth should have a direct effect on how believers live. Because God will change this world as we know it, we ought to live in keeping with His perfect holiness. The thought of the earth's destruction should not lead the Christian to despair, for his life ought not to be wrapped up in the things of this world. Rather, he should work and watch (v. 12). The day of God will culminate in a great change in the earth's shape and appearance, for it will be a trial by fire. The Christian waits for this day in joy, not in fear. The believer joyfully anticipates that the creation of the new heavens and earth will result from this trial. The unbeliever, however, does not face this day with joy, since to him it means God's judgment.

At the beginning of the second letter (1:4), Peter talks about the precious promises of the believer. In 3:13, he mentions the promise that there will be more to come after the world is judged by fire. He is probably drawing on Isaiah 65:17–25 and 66:22. We believers anticipate that there will be "new heavens and a new earth, in which righteousness dwells" (v. 13). Righteousness is not at home in the world today, for the world system is anything but righteous. In that future day, God's perfect righteousness will dwell in the new earth, and believers will share in that glorious experience.

The anticipation of such a glorious state stimulated Peter to make personal application for his readers. Since only righteousness will survive this world, it is imperative that believers lead righteous lives. Peter urges his readers to "be diligent" (zealous) for righteousness (v. 14). Diligence ought to be manifest in such a way that certain qualities will be evidenced in the lives of the believers. These qualities are specified as being found among those who live "in peace, spotless and blameless" (v. 14). True peace does not come through external things. A man may have everything from a worldly standpoint and yet be without peace. Peace comes through the knowledge of God's plans and a perfect reliance on Him (see Phil. 4:6–7). Even in the midst of great calamity, the Christian may have peace that passes worldly understanding.

The idea of being spotless and blameless stands in contrast to the false teachers who Peter called "stains and blemishes" (2 Peter 2:13). The Christian is not to be like the false teachers, but conformed to the image of the spotless One, Jesus Christ. In order to be blameless in the sight of God, one must be in Jesus Christ. The Christian who is conformed to the spotless One will undoubtedly be considered blameless. The blameless state of the believer comes through the work of regeneration. In Colossians 1:21–22, Paul declared that "although you were formerly alienated and hostile in mind, engaged in evil deeds, yet He has now reconciled you in His fleshly body through death, in order to present you before Him holy and blameless and beyond reproach."

The apostle Peter has set a high standard for the believer, but he is able to reach it through the power of the Holy Spirit working in his life.

Peter adds one final reminder concerning the patience of the Lord. Peter noted earlier, in verse 9, that the patience of God was for the benefit of mankind to bring him to salvation. It still is: "Regard the patience of our Lord as salvation" (v. 15). God's patience keeps Him from sending His Son back to the world in the Second Advent. That event will mark the end of God's patience. God is still giving the world ample time to repent.

The theme of salvation was not proclaimed by Peter alone. In verses 15 and 16 we have a beautiful picture of the cooperation that existed between the apostles in the presentation of the truth. Peter's reference to the apostle Paul is truly remarkable and demonstrates the authenticity of the sacred text. It is interesting to note that Peter refers to Paul as "our beloved brother" (v. 15). These words show a beautiful picture of brotherly love and forgiveness. Peter and Paul had not always been on the friendliest of terms. They had disagreements during their ministries, as Paul wrote in Galatians 2:11–14. On that occasion, Paul withstood Peter to his face because he was guilty of causing difficulty among the Jewish and Gentile brethren. But at the end of his life, Peter was able to call Paul a "beloved brother."

Such a state of love and forgiveness would do much for the cause of Jesus Christ in today's world. Peter clearly points out that he believed Paul had communicated the revelation of God in his letters. This reference demonstrates that Paul's letter had been circulated among the believers in the first century. Peter himself probably was familiar with some of them, although we are not told which of the letters he had been privileged to read.

Peter believed that Paul had received wisdom from God, and many of the things that Paul had written were difficult to understand. (The author of this study has always been grateful for Peter's evaluation of Paul's writings. We should not be discouraged when we have difficulty with some of Paul's arguments. Just remember that even the apostle Peter sometimes had trouble understanding what Paul was saying!) While he did not always understand Paul's writings, Peter was convinced that they were to be considered on the same level as Old Testament Scripture. Peter called Paul's writings "Scripture" (v. 16), a word that was used in referring to the sacred writings of the Old Testament. This is an extremely early attestation of the authenticity of the writings of the apostle Paul. Peter undoubtedly recognized in the writings of Paul the same working of the Holy Spirit which he had experienced in his own life. Some were already attempting to twist the meanings of Paul's writings, as they had previously twisted the writings of the Old Testament.

CONCLUSION (3:17–18)

The second letter of the apostle Peter concludes with a warning and an admonition to his Christian readers. In verse 17,

Peter implies that his readers are now without excuse for being deluded by false teachers and their teaching. In light of the context of this chapter, Peter seems to be implying that not only he, but also the apostle Paul, had warned these people repeatedly. His readers already knew the doctrine but they were not living up to it. Peter was warning them again, and he expected them to be able to withstand error. The readers were now responsible to watch and guard themselves.

The Christian must never allow himself to become complacent, because error has many attractive faces that can deceive even the most mature believer. The verb used for "fall" (v. 17) was also used by Paul in Galatians 5:4 for falling from grace and in Acts 27:29 concerning the wreck of a ship. The Christian who "falls" away from the truth makes a wreck of his life. To deduce from this that a believer under such conditions loses his salvation is to read something into the text that is not there.

The apostle Peter admonishes believers to "grow in the grace and knowledge of our Lord and Savior Jesus Christ" (v. 18). He ends his letter as he began it, with the subject of Christian growth. The Christian life is either a life of growth or a life of deterioration. The growth must be both in grace and in knowledge. The knowledge of the Lord, which seems to be the key, will be the safeguard against all apostasy and heresy. The Christian life begins with the knowledge of the Lord, continues in the knowledge of Him as a safeguard, and will eventually culminate in the full knowledge of Him.

Peter's final statement forms a fitting close to this epistle. To Jesus Christ alone belongs "glory, both now and to the day of eternity. Amen." Peter's words emphasize again our wonderful Savior and the eternal glory which will be His. There is no more fitting expression with which to close this study than these same words of Peter, "To Him be the glory, both now and to the day of eternity. Amen."

SOME REVIEW QUESTIONS

1. The mockers who come in the last days will focus their derision primarily on what Christian doctrine?

2. What biblical event does Peter use to refute the mocker's argument?

3. According to Peter, how does God view time?

4. Why has God delayed the return of His Son?

5. What did Peter think of the writings of the apostle Paul? Did he consider Paul's writings to be equally authoritative along with the Old Testament?

NOTE

1. *Rapture* is a term used to describe the event at the end of the church age when living believers in Christ will be "caught up," raptured, to meet the Lord in the air. At the same time, the "dead in Christ" will be raised from their graves (cf. 1 Thess. 4:13–18).

BIBLIOGRAPHY

Barclay, William. *The Letters of James and Peter.* Daily Study Bible series. 2nd ed. Edinburgh: Saint Andrew Press, 1960.

Blum, Edwin A. "1 Peter." "2 Peter." In *Hebrews-Revelation.* Vol. 12 of *Expositor's Bible Commentary.* 12 vols. Edited by Frank E. Gaebelein. Grand Rapids: Zondervan Publishing, 1981.

Cedar, Paul A. *James, 1, 2 Peter, Jude.* The Communicator's Commentary series. Waco, Tex.: Word Books, 1984.

Clowney, Edmund. *The Message of 1 Peter.* Downers Grove, Ill.: InterVarsity Press, 1988.

Cochrane, Elvis. *The Epistles of Peter, A Study Manual.* Grand Rapids: Baker, 1965.

Davids, Peter H. *The First Epistle of Peter.* New International Commentary on the New Testament series. Grand Rapids: Eerdmans Publishing, 1990.

DeHaan, Richard W. *Good News For Bad Times.* Wheaton: Victor, 1975.

Gangel, Kenneth O. "2 Peter." In *Bible Knowledge Commentary: New Testament.* Edited by John F. Walvoord and Roy B. Zuck. Wheaton, Ill.: Scripture Press, 1983.

Green, Michael. *The Second Epistle General of Peter and the General Epistle of Jude.* Tyndale New Testament Commentaries series. Grand Rapids: Eerdmans Publishing, 1975.

Grudem, Wayne. *1 Peter.* Tyndale New Testament Commentaries series. Grand Rapids: Eerdmans Publishing, 1988.

Hiebert, D. Edmond. *1 Peter.* Chicago: Moody, 1984.

_____. *Second Peter and Jude: An Expositional Commentary.* Greenville, S.C.: Unusual Publications, 1989.

Mayor, J. B. *The Epistle of St. Jude and the Second Epistle of St. Peter.* Grand Rapids: Baker, 1965.

Meyer, F. B. *Tried By Fire.* Grand Rapids: Zondervan Publishing, 1950.

Plummer, Alfred. "The Second Epistle General of Peter." In *Ellicott's Commentary on the Whole Bible.* Reprint ed. Grand Rapids: Zondervan Publishing, n.d.

Raymer, Roger M. "1 Peter." In *Bible Knowledge Commentary: New Testament.* Edited by John F. Walvoord and Roy B. Zuck. Wheaton, Ill.: Scripture Press, 1983.

Selwyn, Edward Gordon. *The First Epistle of St. Peter.* 2nd ed. London: Macmillan and Co. Ltd., 1964.

Stibbs, Alan M. *The First Epistle General of St. Peter.* Tyndale New Testament Commentary series. Reprint ed. London: Tyndale, 1966.

Wiersbe, Warren W. *Be Hopeful.* Wheaton, Ill.: Scripture Press, 1982.

_____. *Be Alert.* Wheaton, Ill.: Scripture Press, 1984.

S INCE 1894, Moody Publishers has been
dedicated to equip and motivate people to
advance the cause of Christ by publishing
evangelical Christian literature and other
media for all ages, around the world. Because
we are a ministry of the Moody Bible Institute
of Chicago, a portion of the proceeds from
the sale of this book go to train the next
generation of Christian leaders.

If we may serve you in any way in your
spiritual journey toward understanding
Christ and the Christian life, please
contact us at www.moodypublishers.com.

*"All Scripture is God-breathed and is useful
for teaching, rebuking, correcting and training in
righteousness, so that the man of God may be
thoroughly equipped for every good work."*
—*2 TIMOTHY 3:16, 17*

MOODY
PUBLISHERS
THE NAME YOU CAN TRUST®

1 & 2 PETER TEAM

ACQUIRING EDITOR:
Greg Thornton

COPY EDITOR:
Jim Vincent

BACK COVER COPY:
Julie-Allyson Ieron, Joy Media

COVER DESIGN:
Ragont Design

INTERIOR DESIGN:
Ragont Design

PRINTING AND BINDING:
Versa Press Incorporated

The typeface for the text of this book is
Sabon